D0290650

THE UNFORCED ERROR

THE
UNFORCED
ERROR

Why Some Managers Get Promoted
While Others Get Eliminated

JEFFREY A. KRAMES

PORTFOLIO

PORTFOLIO

Published by the Penguin Group

Penguin Group (USA) Inc., 375 Hudson Street, New York, New York 10014, U.S.A. •
Penguin Group (Canada), 90 Eglinton Avenue East, Suite 700, Toronto, Ontario, Canada
M4P 2Y3 (a division of Pearson Penguin Canada Inc.) • Penguin Books Ltd,
80 Strand, London WC2R 0RL, England • Penguin Ireland, 25 St. Stephen's Green,
Dublin 2, Ireland (a division of Penguin Books Ltd) • Penguin Books Australia Ltd,
250 Camberwell Road, Camberwell, Victoria 3124, Australia (a division of Pearson Australia
Group Pty Ltd) • Penguin Books India Pvt Ltd, 11 Community Centre, Panchsheel Park,
New Delhi – 110 017, India • Penguin Group (NZ), 67 Apollo Drive, Rosedale, North Shore
0632, New Zealand (a division of Pearson New Zealand Ltd) • Penguin Books (South Africa)
(Pty) Ltd, 24 Sturdee Avenue, Rosebank, Johannesburg 2196, South Africa

Penguin Books Ltd, Registered Offices: 80 Strand, London WC2R 0RL, England

First published in 2009 by Portfolio, a member of Penguin Group (USA) Inc.

10 9 8 7 6 5 4 3 2 1

Copyright © Jeffrey A. Krames, 2009
All rights reserved

While the author has made every effort to provide accurate telephone numbers and Internet
addresses at the time of publication, neither the publisher nor the author assumes any responsibility
for errors, or for changes that occur after publication. Further, publisher does not have any control
over and does not assume any responsibility for author or third-party Web sites or their content.

LIBRARY OF CONGRESS CATALOGING-IN-PUBLICATION DATA

Krames, Jeffrey A.
  The unforced error : why some managers get promoted while others get eliminated / Jeffrey
A. Krames.
    p. cm.
  Includes bibliographical references and index.
  ISBN 978-1-59184-283-5
  1. Success in business.   2. Businessmen.   3. Executives.   I. Title.
  HF5386.K832 2009
  658.4'09—dc22   2009013104

Printed in the United States of America
Designed by Adam Bohannon • Set in Warnock

Without limiting the rights under copyright reserved above, no part of this publication may be
reproduced, stored in or introduced into a retrieval system, or transmitted, in any form or by any
means (electronic, mechanical, photocopying, recording or otherwise), without the prior written
permission of both the copyright owner and the above publisher of this book.

The scanning, uploading, and distribution of this book via the Internet or via any other means
without the permission of the publisher is illegal and punishable by law. Please purchase only
authorized electronic editions and do not participate in or encourage electronic piracy of
copyrightable materials. Your support of the author's rights is appreciated.

To my mother

TRUDY KRAMES

who, with her Selectric typewriter
and constant willingness to help,
made my writing career not only a possibility,
but a probability.
I owe you the world, Mom.

CONTENTS

THE UNFORCED ERROR

Unforced Errors

The Great Career Killers

There are great visionaries who accomplish little because they don't attend to the weaknesses that cause unforced errors.

—Larry Bossidy, coauthor of *Execution*
and former CEO of AlliedSignal

UNFORCED ERROR DEFINED

The concept of the "unforced error" is a pivotal one in tennis. Created by noted tennis authority Dr. Leo Levin in 1982, it describes an error that is "committed without a cause." It is, according to one standard definition, "a mistake by the player who hits a shot . . . when the player has time to prepare and position himself to get the ball back in play and (still) makes an error."

In professional tennis, the player with the fewest unforced errors usually wins. The same is true in business.

In tennis—as in the workforce—an unforced error is the fault of the player who misses the shot. In both arenas, the error is made by someone with the ability to keep the ball in play but who makes a mistake, resulting in a loss of the point.

For tennis players, committing fewer unforced errors means winning more matches. For people in business, it means better raises, speedier promotions, and enhanced job security. To improve your game in business, as in tennis, you need to develop the habits that will help you keep the ball in play and on the other guy's side of the court.

If you can consistently return the ball and keep the point alive, you won't need aces. You can just play your steady game, and if you follow the advice in this book, improve your performance over time. Don't worry about that other guy, even if you are in a race to keep your job or get a promotion. Without the knowledge *you* will gain by reading this little book, the other guy is more likely to make the unforced error. Just concentrate on your own game.

One modern-day tennis player with a remarkable story is Brad Gilbert, a player who was ranked as high as number 4 when he played professionally. He was someone who beat players he had no right to beat. Later he became one of the best tennis coaches in the world, catapulting Andre Agassi from number 132 to number 1.

Gilbert is proof positive that a player with less ability can defeat greater players by committing fewer unforced errors. When he played, Gilbert had a mediocre serve at best (and a "laughable second serve"), no great forehand or backhand, nor any killer smash that would account for the many top-single titles that he garnered during his career. His great strength was his ability to keep the ball in play. For that, he was called a "pusher," someone who returns every shot waiting for his increasingly frustrated opponents to make the unforced error. He knew his opponents' strengths and weaknesses better than they did and he played the percentages by hitting the ball where he knew they would be most likely to make an error.

For example, Gilbert defeated a superior John McEnroe in the 1986 Masters Cup. While McEnroe screamed at Gilbert things like "you don't deserve to be on the same court with me, and you are the worst!" Gilbert played his steady game. McEnroe was so outraged with the loss that he vowed to stay off the court for six months.

One of the goals of this book is to help make you the Brad Gilbert of your organization. It will teach you how to make fewer unforced errors, and how to recover from the ones that you do make. It focuses on a dozen common ways that managers trip themselves up and ruin their careers. Some may be obvious, but some are not, and some are even counterintuitive. It will prepare you early for whatever comes over the net and help you to play at a steady, consistent level higher than you thought possible.

As for me, I wear two hats in my professional life. I am an author, having written several leadership books on former General Electric CEO Jack Welch, management guru Peter Drucker, and others. However, many of my personal experiences are derived from spending more than a quarter century as an editor and publisher, climbing the corporate ladder in several publishing companies.

ERRORS KILL AT EVERY LEVEL

In a recent study of men's singles Wimbledon play, in the overall tournament, players who made the fewest unforced errors won 70 percent of the time. For those players who made it to the finals, those who made the fewest unforced errors won even more—nearly three-quarters of the time.

It's not the four or five percentage points that matter, but the direction of the statistic that counts. In tennis, as in business, the higher you go the more likely you are to win by making fewer unforced errors and more serious ones as well.

Unforced CEO errors are often spectacular. Ethics breaches and sex scandals make great headlines. Every move a major company CEO makes is scrutinized by the press, Wall Street, and stockholders, not to mention the company's employees. Fascination with the people who lead large corporations is one reason the rise and fall of CEOs is one of the most chronicled topics in business.

The surveys have been revealing. They show that CEOs who stumble—who make the most unforced errors—are being forced out in record numbers. For instance, in one recent year, an incredible one of every five CEOs was ejected from the top two hundred companies. And according to a Booz Allen Hamilton study, in 2002 and 2003, three to four times as many CEOs were ousted for inadequate performance than in 1995.

Here are more numbers that add fuel to the fire: From 1995 to 2006, CEO turnover was up nearly 60 percent according to another Booz Allen study. In that same time period, "performance-related turnover" skyrocketed by more than 300 percent. In 1995, one in eight CEOs was ousted from his job; in 2006, about one in three was forced out. These are revealing numbers that point to a disturbing trend.

I had always assumed that unforced errors are committed by the least intelligent, the least talented, and the least capable. I was wrong.

For example, take Roberto Goizueta, the CEO responsible for the "New Coke" in 1985. This is the marketing decision widely regarded as the greatest unforced product error in history. But, in increasing Coke's stock market value from $4 billion to $145 billion during his tenure, he created more shareholder value than any CEO who came before him. That exceptional feat and his keen sense of global vision are two reasons he is remembered as one of the most effective CEOs of his day.

The Goizueta example shows that even the best and the brightest make unforced errors, and even the worst unforced errors do not need to be fatal. It's often what one does after the blunder that determines one's fate. For Goizueta, bringing back "Classic Coke" months later recovered the revenue the firm had lost and more.

Goizueta recognized his error and quickly fixed it. There is an important lesson in that: The most dangerous errors are the ones that we don't recognize, so we can't fix them before the damage is done. The unforced errors discussed in this book are ones that often go unrecognized by the people who make them (although not their bosses) until it is too late. Reading this book will help you not only avoid mistakes but also become more aware of the ones you do make so you can repair the damage promptly.

Of course, everyone from the CEO to the hourly paid worker makes mistakes. According to Brian Sullivan, CEO of CT Partners, one of the world's largest search firms, "most CEOs have failures every month. Today's wow idea can be tomorrow's failure. CEOs must be alert to the market, their competitors, and their clients or customers. All three will let you know when you've failed, hopefully in time to correct it. Anyone who tells you they have had a failure-free career has committed one of the biggest failures—lack of self awareness."

Sullivan calculated that there were many CEOs who did not get the chance to complete their second year as chief executive. He figured that because he knew of many CEOs who stayed on more than ten years, there would have to be a good number who never see their third year, in order for the average CEO tenure to be between five and six years.

EXAMPLES OF HEADLINE-MAKING UNFORCED ERRORS

The 2008 U.S. presidential campaign offers spectacular examples of both a damaging unforced error and a victory that was won by avoiding such errors. The possibly outcome-determining unforced error was Senator John McCain's decision to name Sarah Palin as his running mate. At a time when the Republican candidate was perhaps five to seven points behind his Democratic opponent, Barack Obama, in the polls, McCain panicked. His strongest case with voters for choosing him over Obama had been that he, as a veteran of the Senate and a celebrated Vietnam War hero, had much more experience, especially in foreign policy, than the young, first-term Illinois senator. But, despite the fact that experience and preparedness seemed to be a critical issue in voters' minds, McCain selected Palin, a young, inexperienced, conservative ideologue as his vice-presidential candidate. The selection of such a staunch conservative not only undercut a central theme of the campaign, but alienated many of the centrist, undecided voters he needed to carry the election.

Meanwhile, Obama, a junior senator from Illinois and the first African American to win his party's presidential nomination, ran a nearly error-free campaign. First, Obama beat seemingly overwhelming odds to defeat front-runner Hillary Clinton in the primaries. Then, in the general campaign against McCain, Obama maintained a steady, unflappable poise, while his unsteady and inconsistent opponent lost critical points. At a time when the U.S. and global economies were melting down, Obama played a composed and self-assured game without a single unforced error of consequence. The fact that McCain had twenty-five more years of experience in the political arena did not help him at all in those final, critical weeks. The error-free Obama campaign will be studied in the future as one of the best-run campaigns in American history.

NOT JUST FOR CEOS

Some errors, such as John McCain's, are played out on a national or an international stage. The errors that the rest of us make are on a far smaller scale. They seldom make headlines or wreck the planet. They usually affect only a few people and are discussed quietly by a manager or two and maybe an HR person (although rumors do spread like wildfire when those errors are made in public view). This book will deal with all sorts of mistakes, from the smallest unforced error to the most significant.

We all make mistakes, and probably every day. However, most are minor and do not rise to the level of a serious unforced error.

In my vernacular, there are two kinds of serious unforced errors. There is the "unforced operating error" (or unforced error, for short) and the "unforced nonoperating error." Unforced operating errors are more common. For example, making a wrong product decision is an unforced operating error. So is not being prepared for a key presentation. An unforced operating error is one made in the course of doing your job—a call that has a direct influence on your organization or operating unit. Executives at Ford and GM who continued to push SUVs even while gas prices were soaring made unforced operating errors.

Contrast this with Harry Stonecipher, the former CEO of Boeing, who was fired because of a sexual affair with an employee of the company. This was a unforced nonoperating error because it had nothing to do with conducting the business of Boeing or making decisions in the performance of his job. Nonetheless, it was a career shatterer.

Since everyone makes unforced operating errors, and probably often, the key is to reduce the number and the severity of them. This book will make you aware of the areas in which managers get tripped up most often, as well as show you how to become—and be perceived as—a stronger leader.

There are seldom excuses for unforced nonoperating errors. You have to have the awareness, self-control, and maturity to avoid them. Executives who have sexual affairs with employees obviously fail on all three counts. The same is true of a manager who bad mouths his boss in front of a small crowd of his peers in the company cafeteria. These unforced nonoperating errors involve an individual's character, and as the management pioneer and author Peter Drucker taught us, "Character cannot be taught or learned." However, discipline and self-control can help to overcome the unfortunate natural inclination to do the wrong thing.

HUMILITY'S A MUST

Humility will be an important theme throughout this book. That's because humility—one of the most underrated of all leadership qualities—is essential to developing the strength and consistency to avoid unforced errors. The kind of humility I am talking about does not suggest weakness or lack of self-assurance. It is just the opposite: It is the kind of humility that grows out of a healthy sense of self-confidence and that allows a person to admit to a failing, to a lack of knowledge, or to a mistake and then get on with doing whatever it takes to resolve the problem. It is no accident that the chief executives who have had some of the most stunning successes of the modern era, such as Sam Walton, founder of Wal-Mart, and Herb Kelleher, cofounder of Southwest Airlines, have had this kind of humility in spades.

Exhibiting a lack of humility can trigger all sorts of unforced operating errors. Managers who possess an inordinate amount of arrogance or entitlement—simply because of their position—risk the wrath of their bosses and the alienation of their employees. I have worked for managers who wreaked havoc on the people who worked for them. In all cases but one, these managers were eventually replaced or reassigned into other jobs requiring less contact with people. I always thought this was an unforced operating error of its own. While some people can change (as we will shortly discuss), people who are truly arrogant and seem to have that gene firmly embedded in their DNA will not be able to change their stripes. You know the ilk I am talking about. These individuals simply do not belong in an organization where attitude and arrogance can act as a cancer infecting vital parts of the organization. Then you are faced with a situation in which people must succeed in spite of the organization, and you never want that.

Few business books devote much ink to humility because it is viewed like integrity—you either have it or you don't. However, I believe some managers can become more humble, just so long as we are not talking about the truly arrogant people I described in the paragraph above. Sometimes a person can become more humble as she becomes more successful and thus more comfortable and secure in her job and her own skin. But the opposite can happen as well. Success can also breed self-indulgence and a feeling of invincibility. That behavior is a great unforced error that will always catch up to the guilty party. As mentioned above, there is no room for that 1970s-autocratic-style management in the second decade of the twenty-first century.

If you work for such an individual and it appears that he will be there for the long haul, you would be best putting out quiet feelers about a new job. Working for autocratic people is a prescription for anxiety and unhappiness. I speak from experience here: I learned the sooner you get out, the better.

YOU'RE NOT FIRED . . . YOU'RE ELIMINATED

This book is for managers and the great number of people who perform managerial work. These are the levels where unforced errors are most likely to be silent killers.

That's because there is less transparency in operating units one, two, or three levels below the CEO. Another complicating factor is that employees who are passed over for promotions or are "let go" are often not told the real cause for their dismissals.

Organizations often go out of their way to keep the truth from people they ask to leave. That's because large corporations hate to be sued. They hate even the most remote possibility of it. Anytime they are forced to fire an employee they create that possibility, especially if the manager does not have a thick file of documented employee transgressions (company lawyers love thick files).

According to former HR executive and author of *Corporate Confidential* Cynthia Shapiro, companies can always find a way to get rid of people they don't want. She contends that companies have blacklists and that management can always find a way to get rid of a person so that the individual has no idea what "hit them."

Shapiro also cautions employees or managers not to think of their HR departments as friends, allies, or confessionals. As she puts it, "HR's primary function is not to help employees, it is to protect the company from its employees."

If you are ultimately fired, let go, or laid off, you are going to hear that you are not being fired, that your job was simply eliminated. But that's likely a crock. Organizations may "lay off" multiple people at the same time, and all of these people have one thing in common: The organization regarded them as a greater liability than an asset.

Strong, loyal performers seldom get laid off. Of course, a deep and damaging recession like the one of 2009 is one of the few exceptions that can change the calculus: In truly dire times, many companies have no choice but to let go of even its best people. Also, as we will see in chapter three, managers with screwed up priority systems often make poor people decisions as well.

I have witnessed a number of people laid off at the same time. Because none of these people regard themselves as "weak" or as "liabilities," they think they have been genuinely laid off.

Eliminating positions constitutes a much safer course of action for an organization, because it requires no proof of subpar performance of that employee. It's a cowardly loophole, but one that has been forced on managers by legal departments. This book will help you diminish the chance that your job will be eliminated.

EXPLORING THE GREATEST MINDS

This book includes both classical and contemporary cases culled from twenty-eight years of observations and experiences in the business world. It backs up my key themes and assertions by citing examples from the best business thinkers and leaders of our day, including Jack Welch, Peter Drucker, Larry Bossidy, Malcolm Gladwell, and others. It also includes great tennis stories featuring

Monica Seles, Brad Gilbert, Martina Navratilova, Venus Williams, John McEnroe, and others. The results of extensive analysis will shed new insights on today's complex operating environment and will help you to build the skills needed to perfect your game.

In conclusion, this book has two major goals: The primary goal is to help you to make fewer unforced errors. It will do so by helping you to recognize some of the less apparent things that can trigger an unforced error while simultaneously helping you to differentiate between major and minor unforced errors.

The second goal of the book is to help you to focus on building your strengths so that you will have the ability to make fewer unforced errors, particularly the serious kind that can cost you your job.

Reading this book will help you to rethink the way you regard talent and leadership so that you can take control of your own future by raising the level of your performance beyond what you thought was possible.

Each brief chapter is devoted to a different unforced error on the court and then discusses its parallel in the world of business. It focuses on one specific and important business concept at a time.

An "Aces" section will end every chapter and highlight definitive actions that managers can take to improve their game as well as the performance of their teams.

The first eleven chapters deal with different kinds of unforced errors from many vantage points and from various organizations.

Finally, the aim of the epilogue is to transcend unforced errors and trace the evolution of performance-improving books that have made the biggest difference during the last three decades, as well as to reveal the latest research and books that have truly identified what makes someone achieve at genius levels of performance (without being a genius!).

CHAPTER 1

The Ball Was Out by a Mile

Face Reality at All Times

I think self-awareness is probably the most important thing
towards being a champion.

—Billie Jean King, winner of sixteen Grand Slam singles titles
and founder of the Women's Tennis Association

It's the athlete's oldest excuse in the book.

A player misses a return and then tries to blame his opponent by declaring that the ball was "out by a mile."

"The ball was on the line" (and thus in), shoots back the linesman authoritatively.

"Out by a mile," the player insists. Even though the entire stadium and the six million people viewing the game on TV saw the ball hit squarely on the white line, the player refuses to accept reality.

Whether you do business in a boardroom or a cubicle, an unrealistic view of the world in which you are operating is one of the greatest causes of unforced errors.

Several seminal business thinkers have taken on this topic of the delusional manager in one way or another.

For example, former GE chairman Jack Welch's most basic rule of business is "face reality." He urged GE employees to see things as they were, not as they wished them to be. He said he learned that from his mother, and it helped him immeasurably throughout his career.

Sir John Browne, the former CEO of multinational British Petroleum, understood the importance of providing his people with clarity and the right outlook. He also understood that communicating with large groups carried its own set of issues: "It's a big challenge, because the agenda is always shifting for large groups and for their members," explained Browne. "The most important thing a leader can do to communicate is to keep the bigger picture in focus, to set the context . . . to explain or reconcile the complexities that cloud the overall picture of what's important and why."

Management guru Peter Drucker saw a manager's "murky" view of things as one of the great sources of managerial missteps. Drucker explained that managers who spend too much time huddled in their offices cannot get a clear view of the market because they are seeing only through "thick and distorting lenses, if at all. What goes on outside is usually not even known firsthand. It is received through an organizational filter of reports."

The only real way to remedy this is to spend more time with customers, to be out in the marketplace, where customers determine value. That's "the only place that matters," proclaimed Drucker. He also warned managers of the adverse effects of success: "Success always makes obsolete the very behavior that achieved it. It always creates new realities."

DELUSION AND THE UNFORCED ERROR

In a six-year study, author Sydney Finkelstein found that the top two causes of management failure are flawed executive mind-sets that throw off a company's perception of reality, and delusional attitudes that keep this inaccurate reality in place.

People with distorted perceptions create pictures in their minds that are simply out of sync with reality.

Note that neither cause of failure has anything to do with intelligence. Smart managers often make egregious mistakes, and they make them most often after they have become successful. This is because their success leads them to become overconfident about their opinions and their decision-making ability.

Managerial teams who view the world through a shared set of "distorting" lenses tend to engage in groupthink. It is not uncommon for a successful organization to become insular and one-dimensional in its thinking, particularly when it has enjoyed a long period of unbroken success.

For example, IBM, once the mightiest computer maker in the world, missed the personal computer revolution because its managers felt that they knew the market better than the customers did. That led to disaster in the early 1990s and billions of dollars in losses. Things were so bad that IBM's board could not find any takers when it went searching for a new CEO (even Ross Perot turned them down). A firm's management team has to commit a number of serious unforced errors to get into that much trouble.

The CEO who came in and saved IBM was Louis Gerstner. Known as "the snack food king" because he had headed up RJR Nabisco before taking the IBM job, Gerstner had virtually no experience in the technology market. So he came to IBM with few preconceived notions about the market or the "old" IBM. He recognized the company had strayed badly from its prior preeminence. And he knew the road back was going to be a long and difficult one. In fact, in answering a question I once posed to him in an interview, he told me that he had to get the entire company refocused on the customer and the marketplace. In the end, because he was able to face reality, he turned an $8 billion loss into a $5 billion profit.

Kodak is another classic example. For years Kodak was the undisputed market leader in the film industry. By the mid-1990s digital photography was coming into its own, but top management at Kodak could not grasp the fact that a new technology could threaten its profitable film business. It responded poorly and then watched the value of its shares shrink by a stunning 70 percent over an eight-year period.

It's especially important to beware the boiled frog phenomenon: Don't allow yourself to sit quietly while the competitive waters around you gradually heat to a level that kills you. Sometimes doing nothing in the face of an authentic new competitor is the greatest unforced error of all.

THE BOILED FROG IN ACTION

I have seen the boiled frog phenomenon at work firsthand. One example that comes to mind is a publishing company that acquired a smaller publishing house in the Midwest.

The acquired company's nonacademic publishing business was faring poorly. Several of its product lines were losing money. Yet the head of that division did not change any of the company's focus, priorities, or strategies. In fact, he did not seem to really know anything about the finer details of the business. He had no idea how many books were being published in each category (e.g., management, travel, careers) or whether that category was profitable or unprofitable. He was content to let things continue the way they were, even though the business was clearly in trouble.

After the company was acquired, the unit head amazingly allowed the former division head to hang on to his job for a while. But even after a number of people were fired, the beleaguered manager still didn't try to learn more about the business. In fact, he resisted. Ultimately, he left to take a position with a smaller publisher. The business survived, but the clueless leader and a number of his people lost their jobs because they ignored the reality of what was really happening to the business.

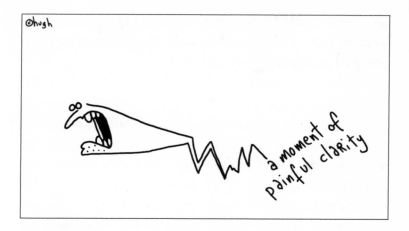

"CONFRONTING REALITY" BY THE BOOK

I can't tell you how many times I have witnessed colleagues making decisions that seem to have no basis in reality. One mistake they make is championing a project that is clearly going nowhere. They throw good money after bad, even though everything in the marketplace is telling them to abandon the project.

I have also seen managers making delusional decisions when it comes to budgeting. I have seen them promise to deliver double-digit sales increases in markets that are growing by an anemic 2 to 3 percent. There was nothing in the pipeline that suggested double-digit growth, but managers promised it nonetheless (and paid the price for it later when reality intervened).

This issue of facing reality was important enough to inspire two of the best-selling authors of our day, *Execution* writers Larry Bossidy and Ram Charan, to write an entire book on the topic, *Confronting Reality*. The book emphasized the perils of making decisions after one "drifts steadily away from realism."

The authors also warned that the problem is getting worse and that the stakes are getting higher. "Many people in business today are boxed in by dysfunctional habits that more often than not obscure reality, rather than expose it. Many have succeeded anyway in the past. Fewer will in the future because . . . the business environment is becoming far less forgiving of mistakes," they wrote.

Bossidy and Charan focused on the business aspects of reality, urging managers to ask themselves and their management teams these questions:

- What's the nature of the game [business] we are in?
- Where is it going?
- How do we make money in it?

These are critical questions that are appropriate for senior managers. They will resonate less with those of us who specialize in one aspect of business, such as marketing, product design, sales, et cetera. Specialists are generally less concerned with sweeping questions like "what business are we in?" and more attuned to everyday concerns such as deadlines, budgets, writing performance reviews, and so on. They do, however, need to face the reality of their own situations.

Bossidy and Charan's conclusion that today's business environment is more demanding and less forgiving is true at every level of the business. Specialists are as likely to be "boxed in by dysfunctional habits that obscure reality" as generalists who are concerned with the business as a whole.

Specialists should be asking questions, the kind Peter Drucker advised the managers he counseled:

- How does my work contribute to the organization as a whole?
- What can I be doing to make my unit more effective?
- What actions should I stop doing because they no longer make sense?

Drucker's last question—about what to abandon—speaks directly to the problem I framed at the beginning of this section about managers who argue to pour more money into money-losing, ego-driven projects that have no place other than in the product graveyard.

POPULAR DELUSIONS AND THE MADNESS OF MANAGERS

What happens when managers see the world through a delusional lens—when their perception reflects something different from reality? They make unforced errors because they don't understand the situation and thus can't see that it calls for a forehand and not a backhand shot. There are a number of false beliefs that often get managers into trouble. Some of these probably sound familiar:

- "Sales will finally take off . . . next year for sure" (although revenues have been flat three of the last four years). I have seen managers in mature, low-growth industries forecast double-digit growth when there is no evidence to back it up. Whether it's ego or a tendency to want to please top management, overly optimistic forecasts are one of the classic reasons for an unforced error.

- "Just give that new product another year to catch on." As discussed earlier, it is common for product managers to stubbornly adhere to the belief that a failed product will soon experience a miraculous turnaround. Holding on to this false future is another common source of unforced errors. The manager who won't accept the reality that a product is a dud causes the company to continue to throw money down the drain and diverts resources from the pursuit of other potential successes. (This example is also inspired by Peter Drucker, who felt that managers had a tendency to hold on to the past for far too long.)

- "I'm finally going to get that promotion." A supervisor who has held the same job for six years thinks her long-awaited promotion is just around the corner. As a result, she makes a great unforced error by turning down an outside job offer. She does not realize that her personal brand equity has peaked and she is not regarded as managerial material. Her managers do not tell her because they have her "right where they want her" in her current position where her performance is acceptable. Her best move is to get out of that company as soon as possible and reinvent herself somewhere else, where she can start over with a clean slate.

- "Even if they do reorganize and cut heads, they will never cut my job." The old adage "no one is indispensible" is true. I have seen even the most talented people lose their jobs during a job cut. One of the best ways to lessen the chances that your position will be eliminated is to have a job that brings in a measurable amount of revenue and profit. These are the jobs that are usually cut last.

- "Employee X doesn't get it, but he'll come around in a year or two." Holding on to an employee who does not live up to the organization's values or performs at a subpar level is cancerous. Jack Welch called trying to "turn 'C' players into 'B' players a wheel-spinning exercise." If a person lives up to the values of the firm, you might give him one more chance to perform in a different position. But if his values are bad or tainted, he is not worth saving.

Failure to face reality is one of the most damaging of unforced errors. Like the tennis player who wastes energy arguing with the judge instead of focusing on keeping the ball in play, a manager who doesn't read a situation correctly is destined to waste vital resources. His own actions will be misguided and he will lead others to engage in unproductive activity. As an error of perception, it is also one of the hardest for an offender to recognize.

ACES!

What more can individuals do to guard against the kinds of delu-
sions and flawed perceptions discussed above? How can managers
develop habits that eliminate the likelihood of an unforced error?
There are a few key ways managers can keep themselves in the game
by facing up to the reality of the playing field:

- *Don't cling to the past:* All products and processes outlive
  their usefulness at some point. Prune product lines on a regular basis. Don't wait to discover that they have been made
  irrelevant by new technologies or new competitive products.
  Analyze sales patterns and trajectories. If there are signs of
  fading, accept it and work with your team to create replacement products.

- *Keep it real in budgeting:* For people with budget responsibility, making your numbers is imperative. Set ambitious goals
  but resist the impulse to overpromise. Build budgets from the
  bottom up. Don't just start with last year's numbers and add on
  to them. Take a blank piece of paper and make a list of the factors most relevant to your markets and operating environment:
  everything from the strength of your upcoming product line
  to external variables such as the economy, the competition,
  and timing of product releases. Involve others in the discussion
  and make sure that you encourage them to ask the tough
  questions.

- *Get realistic about your own career:* Nothing is more disappointing than expecting a promotion that never comes. But you deserve to know your career path options and chances for promotion. Don't wait for performance review time to engage your boss in discussions about your future. Ask her to lunch or out for a cup of coffee. If you are a manager hoping to rise further, this is particularly important. That's because according to the *Wall Street Journal*, 92 percent of managers feel they are doing an excellent or good job but only two-thirds of their employees agree (according to a survey of 1,854 U.S. workers by Rasmussen Reports). You need to know if your boss thinks as highly of your work as you do. If she doesn't, you need to figure out how to improve her opinion of you, or move on to a situation where you will be appreciated.

- *Be up front with your direct reports:* You need them to be realistic both about the operating conditions that affect your business and about their own performance. This is especially important for those who are not making the minimum grade. It is unrealistic for you to expect that they will improve if you aren't up front about their shortcomings. Take them out for a cup of coffee. Start with honest praise about what they do well. Then be as specific as possible about the areas where they are not up to par. Always be honest, but be sure that your tone and your language are calm and unemotional. Tell them exactly what they need to do to turn things around.

Follow up this discussion within a week with a written memo containing the same information. The memo should include specific action items to address the problem areas, with the dates by which they should be completed. You may need to work with someone in HR to finalize the written document. Remember that legal and HR like thick files that document an employee's weaknesses. The goal is to help the employee improve and save her job, but if that fails, a well-documented file will keep you in the good graces of the HR and legal departments.

CHAPTER 2

Choosing the Wrong Partner

The Most Important Call

*If you remember only one thing, remember that doubles is
a little like marriage: nothing destroys the partnership faster
than a lack of communication.*

—Harry Hopman, captain of fifteen winning
Australian Davis Cup teams

According to Peter Fleming, who won seven Grand Slam doubles titles, the best doubles team ever was "John McEnroe and anyone." Unfortunately, most of us don't have the talent of John McEnroe. So we need to make sure that we pick teammates who will be assets to our team.

Tennis players almost always get to pick their doubles partners. In business, you can't always choose your teammates. As a new employee you usually have to work on the team to which you are assigned. But one of the big responsibilities that comes as you rise into the ranks of management is the authority to hire new members of your team. And it is in this critical area, at this crucial stage in their careers, that many new managers make unforced errors.

This chapter is designed to help you make fewer unforced errors in hiring people. I say fewer because there is no such thing as a perfect hiring record.

Every manager makes a hiring mistake at one point or another. Consider it a rite of passage. But hiring errors are very costly. A team member who doesn't do her job well not only makes extra work for others but also eats up the time and energy of both her manager and her colleagues. Especially as a new manager, you do not want to make an error that is going to divert you from giving your full attention to performing well.

A MANAGER'S MOST IMPORTANT CALL

No decisions are as important as people decisions. Alfred Sloan was the chairman and CEO of General Motors for four decades—the business leader responsible for making GM a worldwide force and for defeating Henry Ford in the early to mid-1900s.

Sloan made it a habit to select every GM executive personally, from every manufacturing manager to the master mechanic at the firm's tiniest accessory division. When someone asked Sloan why someone at his level would concern himself with such low-level decisions he answered with authority: "If we didn't spend four hours on placing a man and placing him right, we'd spend four hundred hours on cleaning up after our mistake—and that time I wouldn't have."

Sloan said those words more than six decades ago but they ring true today. Perhaps he was overly cautious. But it's his people principle that counts. Just because we all make bad hires at one time or another does not diminish the impact of the ill-fated decision. Not only do you have to undo the mess that person makes, but you must go through what I call the "corporate choreography" of firing someone (that's where the thick files come in).

Judgment authors Noel Tichy and Warren Bennis agree with Sloan's thoughts on people. Of the three kinds of judgment calls a manager makes—"people calls," "strategy calls," and "crisis calls"— people calls are the most important, they contend. People calls are also more complex, and more likely to be affected by "emotional attachments." And, because people calls are so personal, with "clear winners and losers," office politics often play a bigger role than in other types of unforced errors.

Like all managers, I have had the misfortune of hiring the wrong person and spending hundreds of hours fixing my mistake. All the time that gets eaten away by dealing with a problem employee and the gut-wrenching day-to-day-emotions of the process take an enormous toll on your productivity and that of the rest of the team.

All of the people I have fired over the years have had one thing in common: a liberal amount of negativity. I can scarcely think of anyone I have had to fire—or who quit because they were doing poorly—who had a positive or upbeat attitude about the company and its management team. There is certainly a lesson there for all of us.

First, it does not pay to be negative. If you hate where you are, you need to look around for some things you can like. Another lesson for a manager who is hiring is to screen for negative types and look for eager, positive types.

Second, it always pays to be positive—in private or in public. Even if you think you are talking to your best friend in the organization, do not vent to him. If you do need to dish to someone about the woes in your firm, talk to your spouse or a friend outside of the company. You never know when that person in the next cubicle may be asked for his opinion of the rest of the team or might offer it up on his or her own. So remain positive inside an organization, regardless of who you are talking to or where or when (meaning, even after hours while sharing a drink far from the office).

ATTITUDE AND AUTHENTICITY

Hiring is a tricky business. It's one of the few areas where being too focused on not making an error could lead to missing out on a huge opportunity, and making an even bigger unforced error.

One of the most effective CEOs of the last three decades was the cofounder of Southwest Airlines, Herb Kelleher. He is the leader responsible for the outrageous culture that is Southwest Airlines. I once asked Kelleher how he did it, how he was able to create one of the country's most profitable airlines and maintain a passionate company with such an offbeat culture.

That's when he told me about his rules for hiring and inspiring a world-class workforce. These rules take on greater significance when you consider that mathematically speaking it is harder to get a job at Southwest Airlines than it is to get into Harvard University.

Kelleher was adamant about "hiring for attitude." He felt that people could be trained, and he urged managers to "hire good attitudes even when the people with bad attitudes have superior degrees, experience, and expertise." He also felt strongly that people should be allowed to be themselves at work. No employee should ever have to put on a "work mask."

I have always looked for people with character—individuals with the DNA that allows them to put the company above themselves. That is often the difference between a good hire and a bad hire. People who subordinate personal goals will go the extra mile when the company needs them most.

They are also less likely to sabotage the place with petty office politics. There is nothing wrong with ambitious people who want to get ahead. You want people with a fire-in-the-belly spirit. However, companies like Starbucks and Toyota spend a good deal of time focusing on things like "community," which helps them to hire and keep the kind of people who serve an organization well in good times and bad.

Compatibility is an absolute must when evaluating prospective employees. As Harry Hopman noted about tennis doubles teams, nothing destroys a partnership faster than a lack of communication. You may have the most qualified applicants in the world on paper, but unless you feel strongly that they will fit in and enhance the strength of your team, don't hire them. Legend has it that

> I want to find
> the brightest star in
> the sky and then
> sing to it.

—hugh

Southwest Airlines once had a roomful of pilots applying for a job. The hiring manager asked all the pilots to go into a room and exchange their business suits for Bermuda shorts. Those who refused were not hired. Southwest wants people who take the job (but not themselves) seriously.

SEEK STRONG SUBORDINATES

In researching my last book, *Inside Drucker's Brain*, the most surprising thing I learned was Drucker's feelings toward Franklin Delano Roosevelt, the thirty-second president of the United States. Roosevelt was a hugely popular president, serving four terms of office, and becoming the only president to serve more than two terms (today law prevents a president from serving more than two terms).

Roosevelt, who was paralyzed from the waist down due to an early bout of polio, is regarded as one of America's greatest presidents—guiding the United States through World War II. However, Drucker felt he had one major flaw. He could not tolerate strong subordinates. He was so insecure, Drucker asserted, that he sought to "undercut" anyone whom he viewed as a threat.

Here is how Drucker described FDR a decade after the president's death: "Whether Franklin D. Roosevelt was a great President or a national disaster has been argued hotly . . . for twenty years. But the patent fact that he was a poor administrator seldom enters the discussion."

Hiring weak performers, B and C players rather than A players, is an unforced error that undercuts the effectiveness of your own unit, perhaps to the point of paralysis. Things are simply way too competitive out there for you to go out and try to compete with a team that isn't the very best you can build. Drucker felt that Roosevelt was a poor administrator, and that not having strong people around him was a big part of the problem. You can never hire people that are too qualified or too effective.

Jim Collins, author of *Good to Great,* agrees that there is nothing more important than the people you choose to work in your unit. He explained that when he started the research phase for his book, he assumed that the first step in making great companies out of good ones would be to set a new vision and strategic objective, and then to make sure that the people were squarely behind the new direction.

But he found the opposite.

The most effective leaders made sure they had the best people on board, and any naysayers or weak performers off the team. Only after getting the right people in place could the manager move the company in the "right direction."

Collins added this important point: "The good-to-great leaders understood three important truths: First, with the right people, your organization or unit will be more able to change with a changing world. They will be able to course correct far more effectively than a weak team.

"Second, if you have the right people on the bus, the problem of how to manage and motivate people largely goes away," explained Collins. "Third, with the wrong people, it doesn't matter if you have the other parts right—like strategy and direction—you still won't have a great company."

The key is getting the right people on board first, because if you do, so many other pieces will fall into place.

NEVER HIRE ALONE

Back to Sloan for a moment: At one particular meeting, when it became clear that he and his management team quickly came to agreement over an important issue, he ended the meeting by telling his management team to go back and give the matter more thought. He didn't want "yes men," he wanted to be sure that the matter was studied from every possible vantage point.

In that same spirit, I never hired anyone without having the applicant talk to a number of others inside the company. I always asked my boss to interview the applicant, as well as other managers and employees who would be peers with that person if she got the job. I also had my assistant sit down with potential new hires.

You will be surprised by how much you can learn from these multiple points of view. Some applicants, particularly if they consider themselves stars, may be insulted by having to sit down with someone they view as little more than a secretary. But that tells you a great deal in itself. I always wanted to work with people that treated the department assistant with the same amount of respect as they did the division president.

I never had any ground rules when applicants spoke to my colleagues. They could talk about anything they wanted with that applicant, even if it revealed some of the division's warts.

Every organization has its warts, the things it's not proud of— a dictator for a division head, a poor sales record, a dizzying amount of bureaucracy. Any of these can turn off a potential hire. But that's no reason to hide the information. If that person is hired she will find out about the flaws anyhow. It is better to be honest and open with potential hires. I have had many candidates thank me for that level of candor. I have also never lost someone because of too much transparency. I always felt total transparency trumps everything else.

Hiring decisions are critically important and offer multiple opportunities for unforced errors. You must be constantly aware that your own performance and the performance of all your other team members will be affected for better or worse by each person you hire. A perfect hiring record is unattainable, but you can improve your record if you invest enough time and if you pay attention to a person's attitude as well as to his credentials.

ACES!

- *Use every available resource:* One of the keys to eliminating errors is to use all the weapons at your disposal (ethically speaking, of course). This means engaging others in key decisions, such as who to hire. It also means maintaining relationships with people throughout the industry who can help you when you need an outside perspective. In today's global marketplace, you can't afford to keep anything—or anybody—on the bench.

- *Give potential hires plenty of opportunities to ask questions:* I once interviewed a candidate strong enough to merit a second interview. But by the end of the second session she seemed lackluster, mediocre. Then I invited her to ask questions of me, and that's when everything turned around. She asked many highly intelligent questions and completely won me over. I hired her and she turned out to be an excellent editor. She later went on to become a leader in the business book industry.

- *Don't be afraid to hire people smarter than you are:* Jack Welch said "the smartest people in the world hire the smartest people in the world." You must surround yourself with a talented team of people with enough self-confidence to make decisions without consulting you on every call. Be sure to hire and develop someone strong enough to be your successor. Tomorrow's managers come out of today's good hires. Also, your boss will be more comfortable promoting you if there is a good replacement ready to step into your job.

CHAPTER 3

Sticking with the Wrong Partner

Cut Your Losses

Never change a winning game. Always change a losing one.

—Bill Tilden, the number-one ranked tennis player in the
world for seven years in the 1920s

Breaking up is hard to do. Ending a relationship is always tough, whether it is with a tennis partner, a romantic partner, or a business partner. That is why so many managers delay and avoid firing people. Even after it is painfully clear that a person isn't working out, they make allowances and let them stay.

Not firing people who aren't performing is one of the most common unforced errors that managers make. It is damaging to the organization, and it is damaging to the manager and the teammates who have to deal with the underperformer. A manager who focuses his attention on how unpleasant it is to fire someone does a disservice to all his hardworking colleagues. These are the people who will have to do the laggard's job, clean up his messes, and try to excel at their own jobs in a unit where there is going to be high tension and low morale.

It isn't just new managers who make this mistake. I have seen otherwise competent high-level managers keep incompetent people in place because they did not have what it took to pull the plug. Do not let this happen to you.

Research shows that even senior managers have problems firing people who are hurting the organization, and they often keep people for the wrong reasons. According to consultant and author Ram Charan and *Forbes'* Geoffrey Colvin, "failing to fix people problems in time" is a major source of top management failure. They explain their findings in a *Fortune* cover story entitled "Why CEOs Fail": "Specifically, failed CEOs are often unable to deal with a few key subordinates whose sustained poor performance deeply harms the company. The intriguing thing here is that these executives often know deep in their bones that there is a real problem, but they simply can't move on it. Says one manager: It was staring me in the face but I refused to see it." The failure, say Charan and Colvin, is "one of emotional strength."

Senior managers don't fire the people they should for several different reasons, including these:

- *"He has to succeed."* In this case the senior manager cannot imagine that his number two can fail. The subordinate may be in line to succeed that C-level executive, or he may be that person's protégé. Either way, the manager simply can't pull the trigger.
- *"He's my guy."* In this case the top manager is blinded by his loyalty toward the person. He might have placed the more

junior manager, and their two families may even get together socially. The problem is that the manager is simply too vested in this individual to fire him.

- *"I can coach him."* It is easy to delude yourself into thinking that people can be coached to succeed and can be salvaged. However, that is often a fatal unforced error. Many people just don't have the right stuff for the job and must be removed.

If a person really is a mismatch for the job—at any level of the organization—it never works out well. Eventually you have to ask the person to leave, and the longer you let them stay, the harder it is to fire them. Firing is just as important as hiring when you are trying to build a winning team.

IF YOU NEED TO FIRE SOMEONE, DO IT QUICKLY

As Jim Collins said in *Good to Great*, you can't have a great company with the wrong people. So you need to quickly get rid of the people who are wrong.

I have living proof that Collins's research is right on the money. I was a manager of small teams for most of my career (consisting of five to seven professionals and seldom more than twelve). At one point in time everything came together and clicked. We had a great team. We were blowing away all of our sales budgets and were considered the stars of the company.

But we didn't get there overnight or by accident.

The fact is that for a long period just before our group took off, we were stumbling. Morale was low. We were not making our targets. Our goals seemed impossible.

What changed?

The biggest change was the elimination of one employee who simply did not belong. That individual did not think that he was doing a poor job. He felt that he was doing fine, despite the fact that he was not making his numbers.

I vowed to do whatever I could to help him. I was determined and absolutely committed to seeing him succeed. Of course, with such a small team, everything was played out on a stage that was in full view to all.

I held daily, private meetings with this colleague to make sure that he was paying attention to the right things. I wanted to be sure that he was focused like a laser on doing the things that would help him to accomplish his objectives.

Despite my best efforts, in the end it was a disaster. I deluded myself into thinking that he could be salvaged. He could not. He was not only bringing the team down literally (e.g., we could not make our goals if he could not make his), he brought us down in almost every way imaginable.

Team meetings were uncomfortable rituals. Everyone knew that he was not pulling his weight so they resented him for the unit's ills. After a while, they blamed me, too, for not having the courage to fire him. But again, in a large company, you need a thick file to fire someone.

I got that thick file and put the individual on a sort of probation (with HR guiding my every move), but before we fired him, he decided to resign. His departure changed everything. As soon as he left, and we replaced him, our performance took off. With the right mix of team members, we were unstoppable.

The good news is that we turned out to be a huge success, but I still regret that I didn't move more quickly. The underperforming member dragged down our team the whole time he was there. I don't know for certain if I or any of the other team members would have had more successful careers if we hadn't been held back by this individual. But I do know we could have been a lot happier and we could have delivered much better results for a much longer time.

Of the many people I hired over the years I always knew when I had gotten it wrong, when I had made a bad hire—and always within weeks or months, not years. The longer I delayed in firing that person, the worse things got.

Misfires in hiring often result in a "double fault," or a double unforced error: making the wrong selection in the first place and then delaying that individual's removal once you realize you have gotten it wrong. Once you realize that you have made a bad hire, rectify the situation as quickly as possible. Always remember that you have not a day to lose.

FIRINGS SHAPE THE TEAM, TOO

While not firing underperformers soon enough is the most common unforced error related to dismissing people, there is another one: firing the wrong people. When budgets are tight, companies often try to save money by trimming payrolls. When this happens, it is tempting for the managers who are pressed to do the trimming to make cuts with their eyes focused just on meeting the cost-reduction numbers. This is an unforced error. They do need to meet the cost-cutting numbers, but they also need to to meet the sales and profit numbers. So they need to think about who is most valuable to the company, and who can be let go with the least damage.

In March 2007 electronics retailer Circuit City fired 3,400 of its most seasoned and productive salespeople. The company was struggling financially so CEO Philip Schoonover decided that he could save money by getting its top-paid salespeople off of the payroll. These were people making something like $12 to $15 an hour. The move proved to be an unforced error of the worst sort. Eighteen months later Schoonover himself was out of a job, and three months after that, Circuit City was in bankruptcy.

Building a productive team is not just about choosing the right people to hire. It is also about choosing the right people to fire. And getting rid of the wrong people can be just as damaging as hiring the wrong ones. The big difference is that when you hire the wrong person, you are reminded of it every day. When you fire the wrong people, you don't really think about what you are missing. In the Circuit City case, the people Schoonover fired were the most knowledgeable of the company's workforce, those who could have provided the best customer service at the store level. This is a key factor when you are trying to get people to make an expensive purchase like a flat-screen television. In fact this was the one area in which the company may have had an authentic advantage over its rival Best Buy. Suddenly Schoonover was the anti-Welch, firing his best people and keeping the worst in place (Jack Welch fired the bottom 10 percent every year and looked to promote his best).

If the firings were not a bad enough error, the damage was compounded by the fact that around the same time it was disclosed that the company's six senior-most executives "earned" about $16 million and were awarded another $17.5 million for a total of $33.5 million. Imagine the morale in a company that fires the best salespeople in its operations while its top managers haul off tens of millions. To top it all off, three of the company's top managers, including its CFO and its executive vice president in charge of merchandising, resigned, and at the worst possible time.

It is not surprising, then, that Schoonover called many of the company's ills "self-induced," which of course fits the definition of an unforced error.

Given all of the glaring missteps Schoonover made (he was called "Scoot-Over" by his harshest critics), it is obvious that his own hiring in 2004, or at least his promotion to CEO in 2006, was also an error. From the outside, it's hard to tell if his feet of clay should have been obvious. He had a good résumé. Before joining Circuit City as an executive vice president and chief merchandising officer, he had spent most of a decade in various positions at the number one retailer in the space, Best Buy.

But two things are clear: He was the wrong person for the business climate, the culture, and the job, and the company suffered during his tenure. Which takes me back to my previous point: When you do feel you made a hiring mistake correct it as quickly as possible. Do not be afraid to pull the plug on someone you think is hurting the company.

And take a lesson from the Schoonover episode. When companies get into trouble for any reason (e.g., a bad economy, industry troubles, or specific problems at the firm), don't make this a one-dimensional issue by simply looking for the people with the biggest salaries to cut. People issues are almost always multidimensional issues (think of chess, not checkers).

There is a reason those people make as much as they do, and it usually has to do with competence, experience, and other qualities that your company will need in good times and bad.

Instead, look for places in which people are making contributions that are less important to the company than they were, say, a year or two earlier. Market conditions change, product lines that were once cash cows turn into tomorrow's dogs, and some people who once seemed to really get it do not get it anymore. These are issues that should be considered when cuts must be made.

ACES!

- *Remember the team:* Firing someone is painful for the person being fired and awkward, at best, for the manager who has to do it. But these are temporary emotions. The manager who uses them as an excuse to delay firing someone punishes all the good players who are dragged down by the underperformer. This includes you. The time and energy you spend covering for a poor employee is time and energy that you are not using to deliver results for your boss. Keep your mind-set focused on how the move will help the people who are performing.

- *Be honest with underperformers:* When someone isn't performing up to expectations, tell them honestly and early. Sit them down and be specific. Tell them where they are failing and how they need to improve. Give them benchmarks to measure their progress and time frames to meet them. Keep your part of the bargain by staying close to the situation. Don't let things drag out unresolved. This process will help prepare both of you for whatever comes. If you have to terminate the person, she won't be surprised, and you will have the documentation you need to support it.

- *Look at the positive side:* If someone really is a mismatch for a job, the sooner you resolve the situation, the better it will be for her. To keep someone around when she has no chance of succeeding is wasting her time and keeping her from pursuing better opportunities. In a very real sense, you are stealing this person's future happiness. Adopting this mind-set isn't just a tactic to make yourself feel better. It really is true.

- *Don't fire for the wrong reason:* In all organizations, there are people who work harder and smarter than others. These are the people you can count on. They are the ones who make the best products, provide the best customer service, and go the extra mile. Don't make the unforced error of letting these people go. At Circuit City, Phil Schoonover let the best salespeople go because they were the highest-paid people at their level. He actually targeted his best people for layoffs. When companies close down specific operations, or when they make across-the-board cuts of any kind, some of these more valuable people may get the ax along with less valuable performers. Don't let that happen. If you have a winning player, keep her. Find a place for her and let someone else go.

CHAPTER 4

Overlooking the Wild Card

Developing the Next Generation of Leaders

*Champions are people who want to leave their sport
better off than when they started.*

—Arthur Ashe, the first African American man to win a
Grand Slam event

In tennis the expression "wild card" refers to a player who is allowed to participate in a tournament although technically lacking the necessary tournament points.

A wild card spot is "given to select players who have not qualified for a tournament so they can participate; preference is usually given to young talent in the host country and also big name players who have slipped down the rankings."

I am a big believer in looking for and encouraging "wild cards" in business. Every organization needs a solid team of capable people with a diversity of talents and ideas. To develop such a team, you need to keep an eye out for unlikely players with hidden strengths and create an environment where they can flourish. Failure to develop a strong team of diverse players is a definite unforced error that will hurt both the organization and your career.

You can avoid this unforced error by looking past obvious choices and considering unlikely candidates who may have been passed over by the majority of managers. Then you must give them both the freedom and the support they need to succeed.

FINDING THE WILD CARD

Jack Welch is a perfect example of a wild card.

When GE was looking for a successor to CEO Reginald Jones in 1980, the board of directors considered the forty-something-year-old Jack Welch as too brash, too cocky, and not General Electric CEO "material." Welch was considered so far out of the mainstream that the board did not even have Welch on the list of potential successors. Reg Jones had to pencil his name in.

Of course, GE ultimately took a huge risk and promoted the maverick to CEO. Although his first years were rocky and controversial ones, Welch is widely considered to be the top CEO of his day. Had the GE board played it safe, they would have missed out on the leader who transformed the company and added more than $400 billion in stock market value.

That's why you can't be afraid to take a risk. Don't eliminate applicants just because they have unusual résumés or gaps in them. People might take unexpected paths or diversions from their chosen fields to find themselves along the way. This could be a plus.

CREATE AN OPEN ENVIRONMENT

Over the years I have been surprised by the people who emerged as leaders on my team. The key is to create the kind of environment that brings out the best in people. Depending on the larger culture of the division and the company as a whole, that may be easier said than done.

Informality is one of the keys to creating an environment in which wild cards thrive. Too much formality often means too much bureaucracy, and bureaucracy stifles. It kills creativity and hurts productivity. Jack Welch once said that the part of the GE story that has not yet been told is about the "power of informality." When people are comfortable and not hassled by petty formalities, they feel free to express themselves in a variety of ways.

A good coach lets her players develop their own ways of winning. Some win on serves, other on crossing shots. Let your people perfect their own games. Offer advice when asked or when you can sincerely help, but resist the urge to make decisions for them.

Give people assignments that allow them to shine: In the publishing world it may be asking them to find an author for a particular topic or to edit a particularly poorly executed manuscript. Look for the equivalent in your industry and ask your people to elevate their game. You will be surprised by the outcomes.

Seek out advice from your direct reports. Talk through thorny problems with them one-on-one (you can also do it in small groups, but the quietest of your team may feel inhibited). Asking for their help will boost their confidence while revealing the sharpest minds on the team.

Give praise when it is well deserved. One of the greatest unforced errors managers make is focusing on people's weaknesses rather than their strengths (there will be much more on this in Chapter 8). Make sure that you praise people when they do well. Send a congratulatory e-mail and be sure to copy your boss, the division head, et cetera for the most exceptional achievements.

Provide every person who works for you the freedom and the tools to get the job done. Don't set them up for failure: Set them up for success.

CREATE A CULTURE WITHIN A CULTURE

How do you bring out the best in people when your company is going through a rough patch? Assume that you are the manager of a team or unit within a division of a larger firm. If the tone of the division—of which you lead a smaller unit—is negative or oppressive (for any reason—from a bad sales year to a toxic division head), then creating a positive environment is a challenge.

What you need to do is to create a culture within a culture. You can do this even if you and your team work in the home office. Here are some ideas how:

- *Schedule frequent team meetings:* Gathering the troops in your office, a conference room, or over coffee in the company cafeteria can help. Keep them updated on any late-breaking developments (good or bad) so that they feel they are in the loop. Too many managers make the unforced error of not keeping their teams informed. People hate feeling that they are not important enough to be kept abreast of what is going on.
- *Host regular one-on-ones:* Seek out your people to discuss projects, progress on other matters, and just to find out how they are doing. Invite them to sit in your office and simply talk about anything that is on their minds (nonwork-related issues as well). In fact, sometimes talking about their interests or families can help to loosen things up and help with relationship-building.
- *Keep your sense of humor and use it often:* During the worst times, your sense of humor may be your greatest asset. Your team will take the cue from you. In a bad sales year, for example, when people are afraid for their jobs and futures, your sense of humor sends a strong message that you aren't too worried and that things will be better soon.

MICROMANAGERS DIMINISH

James Blake, the phenomenal, top-ranked tennis player who overcame a broken neck to return to the top of his game feels that confidence is one of the keys to winning at anything: "Right after talent, health and conditioning, confidence is about the most important thing a tennis player can possess. It's the crucial intangible of the game," he insisted, adding that "few people are born with a lifetime of confidence; for most of us it's something that ebbs and flows like the tides. To oversimplify, winning builds confidence; losing takes it away."

The best coaches and managers know how important it is to infuse confidence throughout the ranks of an organization. Unfortunately, I have had multiple managers throughout my career with zero people skills—who focused not on confidence but on stressing people's weaknesses. This made it harder for me to perform well, and in turn weakened the company as a whole. Any manager who routinely strips people of confidence does not deserve to be a manager.

One way that many managers undermine employees is by micromanaging. They don't let their team members make a single decision. They don't let them display their strengths or develop new ones. Often a supervisor isn't aware that she is micromanaging, which makes this classic unforced error a particularly damaging one.

Sometimes the person being micromanaged does not even recognize it because her manager is so engaging or charming or seemingly "democratic" that it covers a multitude of sins. Or the person being managed to death may not realize it because a previous manager was ten times worse.

When you are the potential micromanager, you may have no clue that you are holding the reins too tight. In order to figure out if you fall into this unwelcome category, you need to ask a whole other set of questions from the opposite side of the ledger.

For example, does there seem to be an unexplained morale problem with your direct reports? Do your people shy away from one-on-one conversations with you? Has turnover been particularly high in the last twelve to eighteen months?

To avoid the plight of the manager who can't let go, consider the following steps:

- *Establish parameters with each of your people, making it clear what decisions they can make on their own and which need to be cleared by you.* Reduce the number of approvals required for routine matters in your department. Err on the side of giving people too much rope. You can always tighten things up later.
- *Make every employee a participant, not just an onlooker.* This takes the concept of empowerment one step further by forcing some people out of their comfort zones. This entails sitting down with them and asking them to make a decision on several pending important projects of your choosing.
- *Give people as much flexibility in doing their jobs as your company allows.* One of the key managers that helped to make Starbucks a worldwide phenomenon, Howard Behar, sums it

up nicely when he urges managers to "Let the person who sweeps the floor choose the broom." This is another way of saying give people the freedom, and room, to figure out the best way to perform their own jobs.

In summary, one of the keys to success is to find the wild cards, the hidden jewels who are real difference makers in organizations. Missing out on a potentially great person is a costly unforced error. The best managers know to look for those unlikely great hires, and they make sure there is a culture in place that will bring out everyone's strengths. They also know that creating open organizations in which communication flows freely is one of the keys to nurturing wild cards. They meet with their people often, host team meetings on a regular basis and give informal feedback in frequent one-on-ones with their direct reports.

ACES!

- *Use classroom coaching when needed:* At any one time, a manager will have people on their teams with different levels of experience (especially if you are hiring for attitude). That's not a bad thing, but often requires classroom (or conference room) training. This is a great way to sharpen skills and develop the leaders of tomorrow.
- *Engage direct reports frequently in informal dialogue:* Eighty percent of the training that goes on in an organization does not

happen in formal settings like classrooms (although, as stated above, classroom training is important). Instead it happens in informal discussions in the halls, offices, and company kitchens. Encourage these kinds of talks whenever you can and invite others out of their offices to do the same.

- *Promote people as often as you can:* People need to grow and learn and take on more assignments. One of the classic unforced errors is letting people languish in jobs they have outgrown. That is the best way to lose key A players. Promote people as often as you can when they are ready to make the leap. If jobs are not there, give them regular raises and encouragement.

CHAPTER 5

Not Keeping Your Game Inbounds

Living—and Leading—by the Rules of the Game

For the first few years, I almost never spoke an obscenity to an umpire or a linesman. Then, at a certain point, I went over the line. There were reasons for it—reasons, not excuses. . . . Once I began to go over the line, I should have been defaulted [disqualified].

—John McEnroe in his aptly titled book,
You Cannot Be Serious

John McEnroe is right. His notoriously bad behavior on the tennis court was way out of bounds, and he should have been disqualified for it. The only reason he wasn't was that he was such a highly talented superstar.

Most of us are not so talented, and we aren't superstars. So we need to play by the rules. Your boss is going to judge you by how well you live up to the company's values. So it's up to you to know the values and keep your behavior inbounds.

In all organizations, there is the equivalent of inbounds. The inbounds defines the playing field for managers and employees by determining priorities and what behaviors they are expected to exhibit on a day-to-day basis.

The values of the firm describe the intangible qualities that distinguish one company from another. Think of them as the soul of the organization. They guide the company and its people to act and make decisions in a way that is consistent with the spirit of the organization.

BEING FIRM ABOUT FLEXIBILITY

Some companies have values so unique that they become a hallmark in the eyes of the public. At Southwest Airlines, flexibility is a hallmark value.

Southwest has been the most admired airline in the United States, and the only airline that has been profitable year in and year out for more than three decades. One of its ten guiding principles calls for its people to keep jobs flexible at the boundaries. One Southwest ramp manager explained that principle by explaining that "At Southwest, anyone can do any function, even the supervisors."

That manager explained that all Southwest's job descriptions end with a statement that calls on employees to do whatever is necessary to "enhance the overall operation" of the airline. Examples of this type of flexibility include pilots that "throw bags" and maintenance people who load bags, push planes, or take apart wheelchairs (none of which is explicitly stated in their job descriptions).

Southwest customers have seen this value in action. They have been waited on by pilots at ticket counters and have seen luggage handled by nonluggage handlers. This has left an indelible impression on customers and is one of the reasons the company has earned such high marks from its customers while the major airlines continue to sink in popularity (and profits).

There are consequences for those that cannot live up to the company's value code. A Southwest employee who refuses to play by the "anyone can do anyone's function" rule is making a huge unforced error and will not last long at Southwest.

THE IMPORTANCE OF SELF-CONTROL

However, sometimes value codes are difficult to discern for an employee or manager. For instance, sometimes a senior manager simply cannot tolerate being challenged in public by a subordinate. So not challenging that senior person may be a rule to live by, but you won't find it written anywhere in the company's stated set of value statements.

When such a person speaks to your group, you had better exercise a great deal of self-control. I have seen lack of self-control wreck more than one career and in many cases the person hadn't a clue that what they were doing was killing their own future in that company.

Many of these cases involve how one behaves in a public setting with peers and the head of the unit of their organization.

The most common example occurs at a large company gathering or at a national sales-type conference in which the unit head announces some new important, company-wide initiative. Rather than sitting quietly, and holding one's tongue, I have seen managers raise their hands and ask provocative questions that in essence show that he or she is not entirely on board with that new initiative. The individual asking the question is not aware that he is betraying his misgivings, but that only makes things worse. Given how hard it is to get everyone on the same page, that manager's question undermines the unit head's ability to get everyone to rally around that new program.

Since that (more junior) manager had concerns, he could have saved them for a discreet one-on-one conversation with his boss at a later date. Instead, the unit head now has blackballed that manager in his own mind. Even if a promotion opens up that is perfect for the inquisitive employee, he will never promote that person, always fearful that he is dealing with someone who is anything but a team player. And worse, if a round of layoffs needs to be made, that individual might have just moved his name to the top of the list.

It is always better to be extremely careful with what one says to the head of a group or organization in a public setting, especially when that person is, say, your boss's boss, or worse yet, your boss's, boss's boss. I am not saying that you have to walk on eggshells all of the time, but when you do decide to raise your hand and pose a direct question that relates to a company policy, you need to ask yourself the following three questions:

1. How is this question likely to be perceived by your superiors in the room?
2. Will this enhance your reputation, or risk it?
3. Is it worth the risk?

In my career, I have only taken such a risk when I know with 90 percent certainty that the answer to question number two is the former—that asking such a question will enhance my reputation.

But what if you seriously can't go along with the new program for any reason? Then you can talk to your boss or HR or anyone later, or if it's really something you can't go along with, you can leave the company. But let it be your decision and not someone else's. That way you avoid making an unforced error that could derail your career.

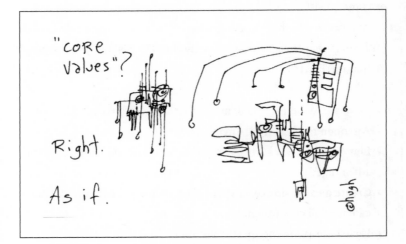

THE HOUSE THAT JACK BUILT

History shows us that the most remarkable companies do have a stated set of values that are known—and adhered to—by the vast majority of the company's employees. They also have leaders who consciously work on shaping values that will help the company succeed.

Jack Welch made values the centerpiece of a company transformation when he became CEO of GE. In the early 1980s he fired close to 120,000 workers, in part because he wanted to change the company's culture and values.

Working with consultants at the company's corporate university at Crotonville, Welch came up with a list of values that he felt would play a huge role in the company's transformation. He was so set on these new "values" that he also added that anyone who could not live up to these values should find another place to work. That was an extreme position to take in the mid-1980s when talk of company values was scarce in most companies. Here is a sample of the values for leaders that Welch felt so strongly about in his first years as head of General Electric:

- Have a passion for excellence and hate bureaucracy
- Are open to ideas from anywhere
- Live quality . . . and drive cost and speed for competitive advantage
- Create a clear, simple, reality-based vision . . . and communicate it to all constituencies
- Have enormous energy and the ability to energize others

Welch didn't just talk about values. He lived them. He embodied these values in his own behavior, and he evaluated people based on how well they did the same. He even publicly fired some top performers because they didn't live up to the values. He said that their out-of-bounds behavior set a bad example and would ultimately destroy the company.

Managing by values is not new. Thomas Peters and Robert Waterman, authors of the 1982 management bestseller that helped to usher in the business-book boom—*In Search of Excellence*—identified eight characteristics of excellent companies. Stressing business values was one of the key determinants of success, they argued more than two decades ago.

Steve Jobs, the cofounder and savior of Apple, Inc., also sees values as a key to his company's success: "The only thing that works is management by values." He urges managers to "find people who are competent and really bright, but more importantly, people who care exactly about the same things you care about."

ALL ORGANIZATIONS HAVE VALUES

It is important to remember that all organizations have values. If you are lucky, the leaders of your organization will be clear about their values. They will discuss them openly. They will live by them, and the values will be productive ones, like respecting other people and paying attention to the customer.

At some companies nobody talks about values, and at others, the top executives talk about having high-minded values but they don't live by them. These situations are particularly tricky. That's because there are real values at work even if no one talks about them. These real values are the ones that determine what kinds of behavior will get you a promotion and what kinds of behavior will keep you on the treadmill.

Despite what management says, or doesn't say, you need to figure out for yourself what the real, on-the-ground values are, and tune your behavior accordingly.

Many CEOs talk about values because they have read the books and been told that they should. But they don't take them seriously. I worked for one small division that spent months coming up with the six values that they felt best embodied the heart of the organization. Lower-level employees were enlisted in writing the values statement—a great idea that makes sure to get buy-in at every level.

However, once the values were finalized and inscribed on pyramid-shaped paperweights given to every employee, they were never referred to again. There was no follow-up and no further communication about them. This sent the message throughout the organization that the announced values didn't matter.

Meanwhile, their real values were still very much at work. One of the announced values was about treating people with respect, but the editors who signed on the most authors continued to be the most rewarded, regardless of how badly they treated the authors after their contracts were signed. The numbers were still all that mattered.

You are making a serious error if you do not understand what the real values of your organization are. It is an error that can lead to making many more, as you step out of bounds without even knowing it.

There are always rules of behavior that define winners and losers, even if they aren't spoken. A good place to start figuring out what the rules are is to look at who gets promoted and who doesn't.

Understanding the values of your company will help you avoid the most damaging error you can make. That is to waste your time, and your soul, in a company whose values conflict with your own.

It is possible, even desirable, to change some of your values. These are the ones that I call "operational" values. They relate to fulfilling a strategy. For example, if you move from a company that serves high-end customers with state-of-the-art technology to a company that serves the mass market with simply functional products, you will need to change how you think about what is important. In your old company, the willingness to spend weeks fiddling and tweaking to get your product exactly right was a highly rewarded trait. In your new company, in order for it and you to succeed, you must learn to accept when something is "good enough" and let it go.

Lining up your operational values with the company's strategy will help you be a more productive, creative, and valued employee.

On the other hand, we all have a complex set of personal values that are harder to change. These values relate to ethics and morals, and how we treat other people. I personally believe very much in honesty and fair dealing, and I think that these should be universal values for everyone. I believe that these personal values are good for business as well.

The topic here, however, isn't what your personal values are. The important thing is that you need to be aware of them, and to know what are the real values at work in your organization. Unless you are the CEO who can fire lots of people as Jack Welch did, you need to recognize that you probably can't change the values of the organization, so you need to adjust yours to more nearly match the company's or look for another job. Otherwise, the moral conflicts will make you miserable every day that you go to work, and you will probably perform miserably as well.

We often think of staying inbounds in terms of our performance at work. Did we deliver adequate results that were in an acceptable range? Did we hit the ballpark estimate? But as important as it is to deliver results that are inbounds, it is equally important to make sure that your behavior is inbounds. You need to be clear about values. To dismiss them as soft, vague, or unimportant is an error you can't afford to make.

ACES!

- *Make the company's values your own:* Your values will affect both what you do and how you do it. If you are a slow perfectionist in a company where speed is a competitive advantage, you will not make the right decisions, and the work that seems valuable to you will not be appreciated by others. Understanding the business model will help you appreciate why certain values are needed.

- *Look, don't just listen:* The values that your bosses talk about aren't always the ones that they operate by. Don't take their word for it. Watch what happens around you. Look at who is being promoted and who isn't. That will tell you what the bosses really care about.

- *Manage with values:* If you are a manager, align your team around a set of shared values. You will be amazed by the results. Be explicit about the values. Talk about them with your team members. Discuss why they are important. Live them yourself. And be sure to reward the people who also live by them and punish those who don't.

CHAPTER 6

Always Playing with a Singles Mind-set

The Partnership Imperative

No matter what accomplishments you make, somebody helps you.

—Althea Gibson, first black tennis champion

There are people who think that they can do it all by themselves. If you are one of them, you are making what I call the "singles error." On the tennis court, champion players may appear to win all by themselves, but off the court they always have teams of coaches and support staffs that help them get to and stay at the top.

The truth is that Althea Gibson was right: Regardless of what you achieve, "somebody helps you" at some point. Unfortunately, many people in the workplace don't realize this. They think that they can climb to the top on the basis of their own brilliance and hard work. As a result, they don't bother to build relationships and alliances that could help them rise to higher levels and stay there longer.

The most effective people are not solo players, but those who work well with others. You can accomplish far more as part of an aligned team than you can as a solo player.

Whether you are a manager leading a group of people or you are the new entry-level employee, you should be considerate of how you work with others. If you help them succeed, they will probably help you succeed.

We all understand the flip side of this concept. If we drag our feet, if we do only the minimum that we are required to do, we can sabotage the work of a teammate. But many people forget that if you are a good team member, you can win the goodwill of your colleagues by helping and supporting them. As a group, you will do better, and individually you will do better.

You may think, "Well, I don't want to help Sheila because she and I are ultimately competing for the same promotion, and there won't be another opening at that level for more than a year." But remember, your job isn't to make Sheila look bad; your job is to make yourself look good. And the best way to do that is to be a person who gets things done promptly and well. It will be much harder to do this if you are at odds with the people you need to work with and a lot easier if you are working together.

The secret here is to remember that you are not the center of the universe. The top executives of the company, the board of directors, and the shareholders probably don't know anything about you. This doesn't mean that they aren't hoping for your success. Most companies have significant budgets for training and career development programs designed to help you gain experience and rise in the corporation. But what these owners and managers care about is not how happy, rich, and powerful you become, but how effective you are at getting your job done and helping the company to succeed. The bottom line is that what they care about is the bottom line: profits.

If you can keep this in mind, you will understand that it isn't your personal accomplishments that are going to determine whether you get ahead. Being a good, reliable performer is a requirement for you to succeed over the long term. But you are going to be judged not by your solo accomplishments but by how much you contribute to making the company reach its goals.

You may come up with a brilliant marketing plan. You may get pats on the back from your boss and applause when you lay out a great idea. But if you can't win the hearts and minds of the people you need to implement it, and if you don't help them do it well, the plan isn't going to work. You may argue that you did your job by coming up with the plan in the first place and that the problem was with the other people who didn't execute effectively. When the plan doesn't work, however, you will get at least some of the blame for wasting the company's time and resources on a failed marketing plan.

Another example: I may put in many hours of overtime, tying up all the IT resources of the department so that the piece of the strategic plan that I deliver will be an audio-visual marvel. But if my self-serving perfectionism hogs resources and keeps other people from getting their parts done, the team will not succeed. This will be partly my fault. Even if the boss looks at the plan and says, "Jeffrey delivered brilliantly while the others didn't," I am still going to lose over time. For one thing, I am still part of a team that didn't get its job done. And for another, I will have many of my colleagues angry with me so my job is going to be a lot harder in the future.

Helping your colleagues doesn't mean doing their work. As in tennis, stepping into your partner's half of the court, trying to take his shots, is just as counterproductive as thinking only of your own shots and flubbing them.

A well-oiled machine is one that runs well because it has a minimum amount of friction. You can oil the machinery of your department by doing things to reduce friction. In doubles tennis, you can come up with a strategy with your partner that calls for one of you to stay at the baseline while the other plays the net.

In the workplace you can prioritize your requests to others in and out of your department or unit. If something is urgent, say so. If something is not urgent, then say that. This will help the other person do their job in a way that maximizes their success. If you claim that everything is urgent, people are going to stop believing you and they will do nothing that you ask for quickly. One the other hand, if something is urgent and you don't tell your colleague, you may be setting her up to make a career-damaging error by missing a critical deadline.

SHARING INFORMATION A KEY

Sharing information is another way to help your operation run smoothly. Don't try to gain power over other people by withholding information. They will be able to make better decisions and deliver better results if they understand the bigger picture. Martina Navratilova once said: "I always loved doubles. I love playing on teams, I love working with a partner and trying to figure things out."

What Martina was talking about was sharing information. She was one of the best tennis players in the world, but she didn't try to order her partners around. She told them what she knew about the opponents and how the game was likely to unfold so that both members of the partnership could do their best. She wasn't just thinking about herself.

In dealing with your colleagues, think in terms of helping them and the whole team get the best result possible. It is nice to know that there are some executives out there who understand how important it is for people down the line to be empowered and to participate in key decision-making.

For example, Chris Conde, the CEO of SunGard, a global leader in software and processing solutions, understands how much the working world has changed. He feels that the role of the CEO must be redefined. He does not see the senior manager's role as micromanaging. Instead he envisions an organization in which employees share information at all levels, with no input from the boss. He sees the CEO as a "conductor," in which the leader "conducts and orchestrates a system." Peter Drucker was the first to write and speak about the role of a CEO as a symphony conductor (or as a head of a ballet company).

"It is very arrogant to think you can make better decisions than the thousands of people below you," continues Conde. "The role of

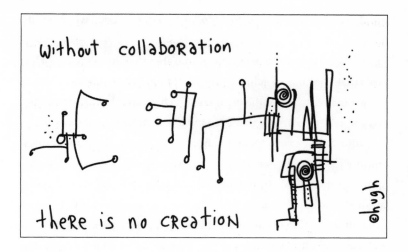

the boss is to make a handful of decisions that cannot be made by anyone else and to maintain the collaboration systems. I really think the rise of these collaborative systems is redefining organizational structures and the role of the CEO; they are the last nail in the coffin of the imperial CEO."

Conde understands that going forward collaboration will be the key to success, and those firms able to move closest to Conde's ideal organization will commit the fewest unforced errors in the future.

BE A "STRONG NUMBER TWO"

Everyone knows that it pays to get along with the boss, but what many people don't realize is that it pays even more to help the boss. Throughout my career I have found that whenever I have the mind-set that my job is to help my boss succeed, we both do better.

I think of myself as a partner, as a "number two" to my boss. He has goals that he wants to achieve. My job is to help him achieve them. It doesn't matter whether the organization chart says that I really am the deputy. What matters is that I see my job as supporting him.

I am a member of a team. My boss is the coach. He has a strategy, and my job is to do everything I can to help him succeed. If I play an instrumental role in helping him to achieve his goals, I become invaluable to him. Also, as a member of a successful team, I will be in a better position to succeed personally. If your boss and your team don't do well, it is still possible to be recognized as a valuable and talented worker, but it is much, much easier to be seen as a winner if you are on a winning team.

Does this mean that you should ignore your own personal performance goals? Hardly. I always memorize my goals as soon as I get them, and at some point early in the calendar year, I ask my manager the specifics about his or her goals. It doesn't take a genius to know that the goals of the division president are the same as the goals for the division.

Good bosses are eager to share their goals with their direct reports. They want their people to know precisely what they are up against, since they know that it is the performance of the group just below them—plus the rest of the troops in the unit—that will likely determine how the year turns out.

In any business, the most important goals are almost always revenue and profit. But if you work in an area where revenue and profits aren't measurable, your team will have intermediate goals that are designed to improve revenue and profit. In technical support, for example, the goals will relate to response times and helping others staying up and running. You need to understand how success for your unit is measured. Then you need to do what you can to help your boss deliver the desired results.

So how do you make sure that you are a strong number two?

The first thing is to acknowledge that being a number two is a state of mind. You are not a solo performer aiming to make yourself look good. You are a supporting member of a team, aiming to make your boss look good. It means adjusting your thinking to encompass the reality that you have, in essence, given yourself an extra set of goals to worry about.

Use your boss's time and resources carefully. This means you should be willing to take responsibility. Make decisions when you can, and only ask your boss for help when you need it. When you do need it, however, ask promptly. Don't wait until a situation has spun out of control to ask for assistance. As Alfred Sloan said about hiring: It takes more time to fix a problem than to avoid one. Remember that your boss's time is one of the most critical and expensive resources of the division. Use your managers' time only when absolutely necessary.

Look for any opportunity to help your boss achieve big things. I am not talking about playing office politics or worrying about minutia. This means that you will have to think bigger/beyond yourself. It may mean subordinating your own goals to your manager's goals when the right opportunity comes along. In my case, it may mean spending time editing an important book that I will receive no credit for but would help my boss and the division.

One of the keys here is making sure that you have no hidden agenda. When working with colleagues to help your boss succeed you can't be thinking "now this is going to help me nab that promotion I deserve." You can't ever have hidden and selfish agendas and hope to grow with an organization. Again, there's nothing wrong with having ambition—without it you aren't likely to go far. The problem is that when you allow selfish motives to enter into your decision-making you are likely to undo all of the good that we have been talking about in this chapter.

We are all, of course, human, and cannot suppress all of our thoughts all of the time. Whenever I felt my brain start to betray me by valuing personal thoughts and goals over departmental ones, I made sure that I recognized it, compartmentalized it, and hit a metaphorical reset button. I always knew that if I conducted myself as a strong number two, then all things would fall into place for me at some point down the line. And that has indeed been the way things have worked out many times throughout my career. In fact, I cannot think of a single instance when thinking and behaving in that fashion has done anything but help me, even during those times when I worked for jerks.

PARTNER WITH YOUR DIRECT REPORTS

So far in this chapter we focused on how you can work with colleagues to make fewer unforced errors. Now we will enlarge the scope of this chapter to discuss how you—the manager—can partner with the people who report to you in order to enhance the effectiveness of your unit and reduce the number of overall unforced operating errors.

Decades ago Peter Drucker correctly predicted that "partnering with the knowledge worker" would be the greatest challenge of the manager of the future. Despite his correct prediction, in many organizations they have failed to get it right to this day.

Although Drucker never defined precisely what he meant by "partnering with knowledge workers," I believe he meant working much closer with your people so that they feel far more like a partner than a subordinate.

One of the key assumptions here is that the old management structures, the "command and control" units that had autocratic managers at the top of the hierarchy, making bad decisions for the people closer to the customers, are badly out-of-date and ineffective. Things move much more quickly today, and people down the line, who actually do the work and serve the customer, must be empowered to make quick decisions.

Many of today's most effective business leaders recognize this. For example, managers should strive to obtain buy-in on company goals by sitting down with each direct report and discussing them one by one. And it is important for the manager to listen as well as to talk. Also, don't wait for annual review time to talk through objectives; instead, talk about goals all of the time in informal discussions, team meetings, and one-on-ones. Be sure to discuss the unit's objectives as well so that each direct report knows how accomplishing his goals will help the organization make its goals as well.

ACES!

- *Think as a team member:* What matters is not your own stellar performance but whether your team delivers, whether it is completing a project on time or making its target sales numbers. You do want to be recognized as a strong, reliable player, but if your team doesn't win, your own performance will be viewed as less effective.

- *Help your colleagues:* Think about what their goals are and what they need to accomplish to be successful. If the department administrative assistant needs to turn in everyone's travel expenses at the end of the month, make sure that yours are in on time, or early. You are going to have to do the report at some time, so do it promptly. Don't make her work overtime, or miss her deadline, because you didn't get around to closing out your trip. Little things that don't cost you more than a few minutes of thoughtfulness can make the lives of others a lot easier.

- *Let your colleagues help you:* One way to do this is to make sure that both of you are clear about what is helpful and what is not. A manager who wants to hire someone, for example, asks the human resources department to find candidates. The HR department can be helpful to the manager by bringing in a string of candidates with real potential, and the manager can help the HR department to help her by being detailed and specific about the qualities she is seeking for that particular job.

- *Rather than seeking "face time" with the boss, do the opposite:* Let your great work speak for you. Don't look to be seen with or by the boss just to be seen. Remember your boss has many direct reports and a lot on his plate. As a result, you can serve him best by staying out of his way and performing your own job with distinction. You need not brag about your efforts; your colleagues and boss will find out about your stellar efforts soon enough, and without you having to tell anyone about what you have done. Be mindful, however, of nasty office politicians. As I discuss in chapter 12, if there are snipers whispering bad things about you in your boss's ear, make sure that he hears your side of the story.

CHAPTER 7

Not Stepping Up to the Net

Taking Ownership of Your Part of the Court

I must keep a strict command over myself!

—Charlotte "Lottie" Dodd, five-time Wimbledon singles
winner, as quoted in *The Tennis Lover's Book of Wisdom*

Charlotte Dodd was the youngest Grand Slam champion in history, and her record has now stood for well over a century. In 1887 she won her first championship by winning the first of her five Wimbledon singles titles at the remarkable age of fifteen. No one has ever matched that record in a Grand Slam singles tournament.

Dodd was also incredibly versatile, as she also played golf, field hockey, and archery as well. To be competitive in all of these sports she had to know something about stepping up and taking ownership of any situation—a quality as important in business as it is in sports.

Not taking responsibility is another of those tricky unforced errors of omission. The problem isn't something that a person does, but something that he doesn't do, so it is easy for him to be unaware that he is committing the error. If you aren't aware you are making errors, you are likely to keep making them and will not take corrective actions necessary to mend the damage done. The unnoticed error is likely to compound, and eventually, you may find that your career is sunk and you didn't even know that you were taking on water.

Taking responsibility shows up in various ways. Some people think that it means admitting to mistakes. But although owning up to mistakes can be painful, it is only the simplest form of accountability. For instance, if your unit's biggest customer is furious because she didn't get a critical delivery on time, and your boss comes storming in to find out why, you have a simple choice as to how to respond. You can tell the truth: that you forgot to submit the order. Or you can lie about it and try to blame it on someone else. Most people do own up to their errors and miscalculations, and it is always best for your reputation and your career to step forward and volunteer that the error was yours. Those who lie are almost aways eventually found out. In fact, if you are a liar, that is one fatal flaw that will surely kill your career.

But admitting to errors is just one way to take responsibility. In the bigger picture, it is more significant to take ownership of a situation or area. At work, people often look at their jobs in terms of tasks rather than responsibilities. But if you don't view responsibility in the broader sense, you may be committing the most subtle of unforced errors: Over time you may fall off the corporate radar screen. Your boss may feel that you are capable of completing a routine task or matter, but if the assignment is more than routine, or if the boss is looking for someone to take initiative, she will not think of you. And when it comes time to promote someone or to draw up a list of the valuable people she needs to keep when corporate belt tightening requires a layoff, she will not think of you.

We laugh at the comic caricature of the corporate slacker who is always saying "It's not my job," but many people don't realize that they do the same thing. How many times have you thought to yourself "Somebody ought to do something about that" when faced with some unnecessarily annoying process, or some cranky piece of equipment? Of course, there are things that you can't do anything about and that really aren't your responsibility, but there are almost certainly many things that you could improve, if you decided to take responsibility for them. If there is nobody addressing a problem that you observe, or taking advantage of an opportunity that you see, think about whether you should be doing it yourself.

Taking responsibility is about developing a mind-set that says: "I am responsible for what happens in my unit. It is my job to help get us to success."

If you have this mind-set, the next time you are in a meeting and your boss's boss asks, "Who is responsible for dealing with Customer X?" you are not going to sit around and wait to see why he wants to know. If dealing with Customer X is your job, or your department's job, then you will say so promptly because what you are responsible for is making sure that the relationship is a solid one. Whatever it is that the boss's boss has to say or ask, it falls into your area of responsibility, so you should want to be the one to step forward and deal with it.

Stepping up and taking responsibility in a situation like this has many advantages. The most obvious is that if there appears to be a problem, you get the opportunity to tell your version of the story. Maybe the boss's boss has heard that Customer X is about to pull all of his business. But what he has heard is wrong. Maybe it is just one little piece of the business the customer is considering canceling, and maybe it is because the customer is changing his product line and won't need that item from you or anybody in the future. Or maybe you decided that you didn't want Customer X's business because he is one of those people who never stops complaining, regardless of what you do for him. He demands rock-bottom prices on everything, and he is slow to pay, to boot. He was eating up a lot of your company's resources delivering very little profit. Once your boss hears this, he will have a different view of the situation.

Making your case convincingly, however, is much easier when you step up quickly and confidently to do it. If you wait until one view of a situation is set in people's minds, it will be much harder to change that view. Also, you can make that case from a much stronger position if you are seen as the person in charge taking charge rather than the person left holding the bag who is now trying to come up with an excuse.

As you climb in the ranks of management, the scope of your responsibility will expand. When I started as an editor, I was mainly responsible for the quality of my own work.

Even when I was at what human resources people call the "individual contributor" level, meaning that no one worked for me, I still had responsibilities as a member of a team. Book proposals that authors sent in would be circulated or discussed at meetings, and although they might not be projects that I would be personally involved in, I had opportunities to speak up. In fact, one of the reasons that I would see or hear about these proposals was that my boss wanted my opinion. If I thought that a proposed book was a good idea, or a bad idea, it was my responsibility to say so.

More and more in today's knowledge economy, companies are paying their employees for their brains and their thinking. Perhaps Henry Ford paid the people on his early-twentieth-century assembly lines to act like thoughtless pieces of the machinery. In today's knowledge economy, however, your boss is paying as much, if not more, for your brain than for your ability to complete simple tasks. Machines can do those. So it is your responsibility to speak up when you have something valuable to say.

When you move into management, you become responsible for the work of other people. Like the parents of older children and teenagers, you are responsible for helping them to do well and also for repairing the neighbor's window when they hit a baseball through it. When I began to have other editors working for me, it was my responsibility to make sure that the work they did—the work getting delivered out of my unit—was high quality. Sometimes this meant that I needed to fix it, but I could only do that to a limited extent. I had hired them to do the work well, and if they weren't doing it, I needed to take responsibility first for getting them help. Then, if that didn't work, it was my responsibility to replace them.

This is where managers, especially new ones, often fall down. Instead of saying: "It is my responsibility to get Nancy fixed, or I need to get rid of her," they fall into a victim's mentality. They complain to their friends that they are overworked and that they are being dragged down because Nancy can't or won't do her job well.

In business, as in other parts of life, we all must take responsibility for our own actions. So, as Nancy's manager, it isn't my fault that she is not a competent editor. But it is my responsibility to keep that fact from hurting my company. If I just sit back and complain, I am not being the responsible manager that my boss needs me to be.

A manager's responsibility is to make her unit perform as well as she possibly can. Beyond making sure that she has qualified personnel, this means establishing work processes that help them do their best. If unnecessary approvals and other little bureaucratic procedures eat up time that they could better direct at doing their jobs, it is the manager's job to change the rules, or get them changed. She may even need to completely rearrange the flow of work or rebuild lines of authority.

CREATIVE ABANDONMENT

The manager who takes responsibility, or ownership, of her unit will look beyond the walls of her department or unit to ask the question: Even if I can get my team to the very peak of performance, am I getting them to perform a function that is truly worthwhile that will add value to the organization? Is an old line of business now dead? Or is one I have been pursuing a dead end?

Peter Drucker thought that was one of the critical questions leaders have to face. "When do you stop pouring resources into things that have achieved their purpose?" he asked. "The most dangerous traps for a leader are those near-successes where everybody says that if you just give it another big push it will go over the top. One tries it once. One tries it twice. One tries it a third time. But by then it should be obvious this will be very hard to do. So I always advise: Don't tell me what you're doing. Tell me what you stopped doing."

In his book *The Leadership Engine,* Noel Tichy (with Eli Cohen) offers a perfect example of this. Leaders must have the courage to change core, fundamental elements of their businesses—that is, their product lines or their economic models—if the ones they had been pursuing no longer seemed to be the best, says Tichy.

To illustrate someone doing this, he talked about Debra Dunn, who at the time was a young general manager in Hewlett-Packard's test and measurement business. What she said has always stuck with me. She was talking about a line of business that she had championed and had personally worked really hard on, but ultimately killed. First, she explained that she had to face reality (think of chapter 1): "I had been involved in building the business (for the two years). . . . I had spent lots of time with . . . all of our key customers, and I liked this business. When you invest a lot (of personal energy) it's very painful to walk away from. . . . I didn't like the conclusion. But that didn't cause me to deny it or hide from it or pretend that reality is different than it is. . . . It was very difficult, but it's what I had to do."

Later, she talked about how she approached the situation. This is where her sense of ownership and responsibility jumped out. Once she saw the reality that the business wasn't going to fly, she said she began to think: "If you just envision continuing in the path that you're on, you see that it's really unfair to the people (on my team) who are invested and committed. I think I need to lead these people to success. And, if we're not on a path that can be successful, then I have to get us on a different path. . . . I have to be willing to say, 'You know, I appreciate your endurance and I empathize with your emotional investment in this business, but this doesn't make sense. Here is why it doesn't make sense. And we're not doing it anymore.'"

Dunn's simple statement "I need to lead these people to success" says it all. She was taking the kind of responsibility that sets winners apart and makes them valuable to their organizations. The call that Dunn made was a big one, but you don't need to be a top executive to step up and take responsibility. The more responsibility you are willing to take, the more likely you are to be valued, and to be given more. Refusing to accept responsibility is an unforced error that sends the message to your employer that you are unwilling to be part of the solution, and on a perhaps unspoken level, that you are part of the problem.

ACES!

- *Keep in mind that responsibility is an opportunity:* Remember that responsibility is not the same as blame. Taking responsibility sometimes requires that you take the blame, but when you have responsibility, you have the opportunity to change things and have an impact. If you don't reach for the shot, you are, in effect, proclaiming yourself to be someone who has no responsibilities, which is to say, no value. Or worse, you may be declaring yourself to be an "irresponsible" person.
- *Think about responsibility broadly:* When you think of your job and your responsibilities, don't think narrowly, in terms of tasks. Think about the larger goals of the company and what you want to accomplish. As an entry-level book editor, my task was to edit the books I was assigned. But a well-edited book on a boring or unimportant topic is still a book on a boring or uninteresting topic. When I accepted responsibility for delivering books that readers would want to read, I became more valuable to my boss.

- *Don't play the blame game:* If there is a problem, never engage in finger pointing and trying to blame someone else. This is just a waste of time and energy and goodwill. The other guy is probably not going to accept responsibility—if he were that type, he would have done it already—so any resources you spend trying to pin the tail on him will be wasted. Even if it was his fault, don't worry about it. You will be admired for taking responsibility for the solution.

CHAPTER 8

Working on Your Backhand

Why Focusing on Strengths, Not Weaknesses, Wins Games

Winning breeds winning.

—Pete Sampras, winner of fourteen Grand Slam titles

John McEnroe once said sardonically that his greatest strength is that he has no weaknesses.

On a more serious note, Mark McCormack, the former CEO and chairman of International Management Group (a worldwide management firm that manages top athletes and sports figures), once said: "Skill and confidence are not the only determining factors [in winning]—the champion's edge exists solely in the mind. He uses any success as a spur to greater ambition; he has the ability to peak when the stakes are the greatest; and he has what is known as the killer instinct."

McCormack said that in *Racquet* magazine in order to equate the traits of top athletes to those of successful businesspeople.

Those who have the killer instincts and peak when the stakes are the highest know something about building on strengths and focusing on the right things.

In business, however, many people focus on the wrong things. They focus on hopes instead of reality. They focus on their own success and not the success of the organization. And they focus on getting better at things they do the worst.

This last one may sound counterintuitive. After all, this is a book intended to help you make fewer mistakes, so logic would dictate that fixing the weakest areas would help you avoid unforced errors. But research shows that the key to success lies not in trying to overcome your weak areas but in making your strong areas even stronger.

The most effective people are the ones who stand out in at least one area. So it is an unforced error to spend your time trying to get better in an area where you are never going to be better than adequate when you could spend your time more wisely polishing to perfection a skill you already have. Work on improving the areas where you show the most promise.

Focusing on strengths does not mean making believe that your weaknesses do not exist, "but managing around them." People who manage around their weaknesses have the wisdom to know what to do, "and also what they should avoid," argued Peter Drucker. When delegating assignments, they keep for themselves the jobs they will do best and assign the jobs they won't do so well, hopefully to people who will do them better.

At University of Toyota, for example, managers are not permitted to discuss anything negative about their employees in a performance review, that is, not unless the employee brings up the topic first. Instead, they are taught to focus on strengths and manage around weaknesses.

Drucker was the first modern-day author to address this critical topic: "Waste as little effort as possible on improving areas of low competence," he urged. "It takes far more energy and far more work to improve from incompetence to low mediocrity than it takes to improve from first-rate performance to excellence. . . . The energy and resources—and time—should instead go into making a competent person into a star performer."

Drucker figured these things out intuitively. But now, decades later, we have a voluminous amount of research to back it up.

Gallup Organization writers Marcus Buckingham and Donald Clifton, authors of the book *Now, Discover Your Strengths,* had a great deal of data to work with in conducting their research on "strengths theory." Their data was compiled from in excess of 1.7 million employees from more than one hundred companies in sixty-three countries.

They define strength as a "near-perfect performance in an activity." Their litmus test for a genuine strength is something that one can do "repeatedly, happily and successfully."

As leading examples of strengths they talk of Bill Gates's genius at taking innovations and transforming them into user-friendly applications, as well as "Cole Porter's ability to carve the perfect lyric."

"THE HALO EFFECT"

Other pertinent research for this book comes from two authors I have known and worked with for years—John Zenger and Joseph Folkman. In the interest of full disclosure, I edited their noteworthy book *The Extraordinary Leader*, among others.

Even though they studied fewer people than did Buckingham and Clifton, they did have an enormous research pool, two hundred thousand 360-degree assessments involving twenty thousand leaders.

These types of assessments are performance reviews that are prepared by several people who surround a manager, including her peers, direct reports, boss (or bosses), et cetera. The thinking behind these reviews is that they reveal more about an individual than do the business-as-usual reviews filled out only by the person's boss.

Their results showed that being perceived as a strong manager depended upon enhancing strengths, not fixing weaknesses (the only exception is in fixing fatal flaws, which we will deal with later in the chapter).

According to Zenger and Folkman, there is a "halo effect"— a person who demonstrates great strength in two or three areas is perceived by others to be strong in all areas. In other words, their weaknesses are overlooked when they have notable strengths.

They contrasted the top 10 percent with the bottom 10 percent and found that managers who had no real perceived strength were rated in the bottom third of all managers in their organization.

However, if a manager was perceived to have even one area of strength, that manager's rating doubled—from the thirty-fourth percentile all the way up to the sixty-eighth percentile (one hundredth percentile being perfect). That's quite remarkable. If someone was seen as having just a single strength, he catapulted his perceived effectiveness by thirty-plus percentage points.

If the leader was perceived as possessing three strengths, his rating soared to the eighty-fourth percentile, and five areas of strength put one into the ninety-first percentile of perceived effectiveness. The most important message from all of this research is a simple but powerful one: To be viewed as a strong player, one only had to be seen as having a few key strengths. "Be good at 3 or 4 things, not 34 things," say Zenger and Folkman.

KEY STRENGTHS TO FOCUS ON

Examples of the competencies or strengths identified by Zenger and Folkman include good problem-solving skills, a strong set of personal values, and broad strategic thinking that goes beyond tactical issues. Other key strengths include:

- Displaying high integrity
- A focus on results
- Communicating powerfully and prolifically
- Inspiring and motivating others to high performance
- Building relationships

- Developing others
- Championing change

What does this mean for you? It means your focus should not be in playing defense, hunkering down and trying to go unnoticed. In fact, that can be an unforced error in itself, as we will see when we address fatal flaws. Instead, enhancing your strengths—qualitatively and quantitatively—will help you to be perceived as a strong leader. The most effective leaders—by focusing on what they do best—will naturally make fewer unforced errors. And if and when they do make a misstep the impact will be diminished. In other words, the stronger leader can afford a minor unforced error or two since he or she is already perceived as being that much stronger than his or her peers.

FATAL FLAWS: THE ULTIMATE
UNFORCED ERRORS

While the focus of this chapter has been exclusively on enhancing strengths, there is one aspect of dealing with weaknesses that must be addressed. Zenger and Folkman make it clear that the worst kind of weaknesses, what they refer to as "fatal flaws," must be addressed.

Put another way, whereas focusing on improving your strengths is the best overall strategy, there are some weaknesses that you cannot afford to ignore. These are the so-called fatal flaws, the career killers. If you have a fatal flaw, no amount of brilliance in another area can make up for it. You have to address it. Many fatal flaws are obvious: a deficiency in character—honesty, integrity. A person who lies, steals, or cheats is obviously not a good leader and will eventually be found out. These are not the kind of fatal flaws that can be taught or learned.

However, there are less blatant fatal flaws, as identified by Zenger and Folkman, also capable of killing a career. And these are weaknesses that you can overcome with effort and attention. Having any of these five qualities can spark any number of unforced errors, and serious ones at that:

1. *An inability to learn from mistakes:* Two researchers, Morgan
   W. McCall and Michael M. Lombardo, examined why some
   executives failed while others thrived. They found that
   some executives not only did not learn from mistakes, they hid
   them. Conversely, the executives who were promoted readily

discussed their missteps, learned from them, and moved on. This one flaw was the single biggest cause of failure. They speculate that not being able to learn from past errors may stem directly from an inability to face reality, which is consistent with the research of Finkelstein, as discussed in chapter 1.

2. *Lack of core interpersonal skills and competencies:* Zenger and Folkman cite two types of failures in this area: sins of commission and sins of omission. People in the former category are autocrats who bark orders, scream at employees, bully their way through the company—you get the idea. Again, this is a type of behavior that is very difficult to teach or change. Sins of omission include people who simply lack the social skills to operate effectively in an organization. They cannot engage employees effectively (they don't make eye contact, do not listen, etc.). They do not offer constructive criticism or praise employees. They are socially deficient and it shows.

3. *A lack of openness to new ideas:* This quality is an innovation killer. Leaders who stick to the status quo are classic cases of the old-style, pre-Jack Welch manager. Welch felt that this quality—an openness to new ideas regardless of their source—was essential. There is simply no room in organizations for people who cling to the past. As Welch once said, "the hero is the one with the new idea." Welch killed NIH, or "not invented here," the arrogant quality that dictated that if something was not invented at GE it wasn't worth learning. Instead, he created a learning organization in which it was everyone's responsibility to bring in new ideas.

4. *A lack of accountability:* Peter Drucker felt that responsibility
   was a prerequisite to leadership: "a leader [must] see leadership
   as RESPONSIBILITY rather than rank and privilege. When
   things go wrong—and they always do—they do not blame others," asserted Drucker. The effective manager takes responsibility for his own team and subordinates and takes responsibility
   by accepting criticism from his bosses. They do not put personal desires above the good of the group, equating the success
   of their teams with their own success.

5. *Lack of initiative:* This applies to someone who simply cannot
   execute. Managers who lack this essential quality fail to make
   things happen and they fail to produce. They do not initiate or
   champion new projects and often sit back. Failure to act or
   execute could be the ultimate unforced error since it ensures
   that nothing gets done.

Generally these five qualities represent something that a manager
or employee does not do (as opposed to something that they do).
This is important because we generally think of unforced errors as
something that is done wrong; here we have five possible sources of
unforced errors emanating from something that is not done.

The key question: How can these be fixed?

As stated earlier, deficiencies in character are nearly impossible to
remedy. However, on these five points, Zenger and Folkman feel that
there is hope. The first step is making sure that the individual is made
aware of that particular flaw. Once an employee knows that there is
a problem in a particular area, he or she can begin to make improve-

ments. But the company also has a larger role to play. The company has a responsibility to "provide developmental experiences that will provide a positive path to remedy dysfunctional behavior," explains Zenger and Folkman. They suggest management-development programs or "massive doses of feedback" as starting points to help these people recognize their own deficiencies so that they can begin the process of reversing these toxic behaviors.

ACES!

- *Make sure you know your own strengths:* This is easier said than done. Many people do not know their strengths or do not use them. Ask for detailed feedback from bosses and peers (this is where a 360-degree assessment could help). Take notes and write your own strengths audit. You want to be sure that you are aware of your strengths and that you are well placed to use them in your current position.
- *Learn and document the strengths of your direct reports:* A big part of being a manager is placing people in jobs where they can make the greatest contribution. To do this you must have a strong sense of the strengths of your people. Keep a profile of your direct reports and add to it as you recognize additional strengths. Make adjustments in assignments as necessary based on the feedback that you glean from your people.
- *Be bold—don't hunker down and play defense:* One of the ways to be perceived as a strong leader is to build up your strengths.

This does not mean hiding your weaknesses. It means developing in those areas in which you already show definite signs of strength, whether that be in communication, in team-building, or in developing talent. The key is beefing up those strengths, not hiding or sweeping under the rug those deficiencies you are most concerned about.

CHAPTER 9

Not Getting Enough from Your Coaches

Why Learning Is Such a Critical Success Factor

Champions are not born. They are made.

—Bill Tilden, from *The Art of Lawn Tennis*

Professional tennis players go to extraordinary lengths to learn their craft. Steffi Graf, born in Mannheim, Germany, begged her father to let her play tennis at the astonishing age of three. She was too small to hold a regular tennis racket so her father had to saw off the handle of an old racket. A string stretched between two chairs in the living room served as a net. When too many lamps were smashed, they moved the game to the basement and used an old couch as a net.

When Graf was five her game saw sunlight and a real court, where she promptly defeated all of the eight-year-olds in the area.

At age six she won her first tournament. Her father was amazed at Steffi's incredible focus as she learned the game: "She did not hit the ball and then look around at other things. She was always watching the ball until it was not in play anymore," he said.

Her focus and concentration, coupled with a fire-in-the-belly enthusiasm to always get better, helped her to turn professional four months after her thirteenth birthday.

Steffi Graf's single-minded pursuit of her goal is extraordinary. Few people make that kind of commitment at age three and stick with it. There is, however, a very important lesson in Steffi's example. Learning and making a commitment to continuous improvement are requirements for success. Whether you want to be a successful manager or a successful tennis star, you need to remember that the people who win are the ones who grow. If you want to be a winner, you have to be willing to grow. You have to be a learner.

LEARNING IS A TWO-WAY STREET

There has been a great deal of research in the past two decades on the importance of learning in organizations. There are many books on the topic about how organizations need to educate their workforces. Peter Senge of MIT, one of the real pioneers in learning and organizations, once declared, "Only those companies that strive to become learning organizations will be prepared to cope with radical change and succeed in the twenty-first century." The organizations that emphasize learning, at every level, have the best chance to succeed.

This is true, but it is only half the equation. The other half, which is often underplayed, is the need for individuals to always be learning.

Anyone who isn't constantly looking to acquire new skills, ideas, and information makes a serious unforced error. This is true regardless of what your position is on the company's organization chart. Not being an avid learner is an unforced error that leads to other unforced errors. When we have an insufficient knowledge base, or we don't consistently learn new and better ways of doing things, we make costly mistakes.

This is true in almost every profession. No patient wants a doctor who graduated from medical school twenty years ago and hasn't kept up with the latest advancements in medicine. And no results-oriented boss wants to promote someone who doesn't know what is going on in the world and just keeps doing things the same old way. That's why it is so essential for you to adopt a learning mind-set.

One business leader who understood the importance of a learning mind-set and continuous improvement in organizations is Roger Enrico, the former CEO of PepsiCo, For years Enrico would host groups of "up and coming managers" at his western ranch to talk and "brainstorm" ideas and business and goals: "There are two things I try to get across," he told author Jeffrey Garten. "You know this question about whether you're born with leadership skills or you learn them? I want them to believe that however you got it, if you practice and work on it, you can become better at it." (There is much more on this in the epilogue of this book.)

"And the second thing I want them to walk away with is that

there's no mystery about how this corporation is run," explained Enrico. "No one is on a pedestal. If there is such a thing as a club, then they are in it. During the week I spend two one-on-one sessions with each of the participants where we can talk about anything they want including their career, their life."

LEAVE NO STONE UNTURNED IN MASTERING YOUR POSITION

Learning isn't just about acquiring skills and facts. Of course, you need to keep your skills up-to-date and to acquire new ones in order to advance. You also need to know as much as you can about what is going on both outside and inside in your company that may affect your work. But having a learning mind-set is about more than that. It is about constantly scanning the world around you for ideas or information that may help you do your job better. And it is about changing what you do or how you do it in response to the input that you get.

"Asking a lot of questions opens new doors to new ideas, which ultimately contributes to your competitive edge," says Michael Dell, who started the business that became computer giant Dell, Inc., in his college dorm room. His basic approach, he says, is "to get to the guts of why things happen" so he can figure out how to improve his game.

The biggest obstacle to learning is a closed mind. It is thinking that you already know it all. Managers who think they know it all are sometimes the prickly autocrats who issue orders and listen to no one. But autocrats aren't the only people with closed minds. A manager who goes through the motions of holding meetings and letting people talk but doesn't ever change anything as a result probably has a closed mind. Ditto the cocky solo player in the next cubicle who never takes a suggestion or an instruction. Even the bored guy in the cubicle on the other side is guilty. They all think that they know everything so there is nothing to learn.

New managers are often tempted to prove that they know what they're doing by taking a commanding, charge-ahead attitude. That is one of the biggest mistakes a new manager can make. If you are new in a job, there are a lot of things that you don't know because you are new. Even if you have been promoted from within the department and you know all the people, you are now in a new position and you have a new relationship to the people who used to be your peers. This is the moment when you have the greatest need to be a learner.

ASK DIRECT REPORTS FOR THEIR IDEAS

It is not wimpy to ask the members of your team what areas they think most need to be improved and what they think are the most pressing issues. It is smart to make use of the eyes, ears, and brains of everyone. There may be people who want to test you and will try to take advantage of your willingness to listen. But it doesn't take long to figure out who is giving you good ideas and who isn't. And if there are people trying to take advantage of you, it's best that you find out early so you can consider whether they are people you want on your team.

A person with an open mind always assumes that there may be a better idea out there. So she takes in everything. She accepts that even the ideas and assumptions that have led to success in the past may not be the best ones for today. If you are open to this possibility, you will be much better able to react to, even anticipate, changes in the future and to take appropriate action. As Michael Dell put it, "Information in its raw form doesn't present itself in neat and tidy packages. . . . Random bits of information . . . won't always lead you to the answer, but they will assist you in focusing in on an emerging problem, or opportunity or new idea."

It is also a good moment to start embedding the learning mind-set in your team. There are four characteristics of a learning organization. Whether you lead a small team, a unit, or a division, it is important that you know how to create and foster a learning culture. In an authentic learning organization:

1. *Information is shared and accessible:* The best companies make sure that information is made available to everyone, usually through the company intranet. For example, as we will learn in chapter 10, Google is a model organization when it comes to sharing information. On a smaller scale, it is even easier to make sure that all relevant information and data is shared with all team members.

2. *Learning is underscored and valued:* As the leader of a unit, it is important that you let everyone know that learning is

something high on the priority list. It is also important that people know that it is not someone else's job but *their* job to bring in new ideas from inside and outside the company (e.g., from mentors, competitors, vendors, etc.). It is critical for you to lead by example by bringing in and sharing new ideas, articles, and so on, so that all of your people know that this is a topic that you take very seriously.

3. *Nobody is punished for mistakes or failures:* This is a critical part of a learning culture. As a manager, you cannot punish people when they make a mistake while learning or trying out new things. This may seem like the ultimate irony in a book designed to help you make fewer unforced errors, but as stated earlier, people will always make mistakes. The key is to make sure that they are not career-ending or huge mistakes. In a learning organization these "failures" will pay off. Mistakes are a big part of learning. For example, when Thomas Edison was asked how many times he failed in trying to invent the lightbulb, he reportedly responded: "I have not failed 1,000 times. I have successfully discovered 1,000 ways to NOT make a light bulb."

4. *People are expected to make learning an integral part of their jobs:* Learning cannot be a one-time thing but an important part of the company culture. People must know that it is their jobs to learn, to constantly monitor the environment, and to bring in new ideas. One way to encourage this is to celebrate new ideas. When someone brings in a new, great idea, make sure that person is given credit in a public fashion. People love

to be praised when they genuinely deserve it. (A form of these four characteristics of a learning organization appeared in my earlier book *What the Best CEOs Know*.)

BE A TEACHER

Leadership consultant and author Noel Tichy points out that most great leaders are both avid learners and dedicated teachers. The best organizations, he says in *The Cycle of Leadership,* are not learning organizations, but teaching organizations, in which "everyone teaches, everyone learns and everyone gets smarter every day."

In fact, says Tichy, winning leaders manage their organizations by teaching. They teach their business ideas, their goals, and their plans for achieving them to their subordinates, and they actively seek the subordinates' input on how to do things better.

The beauty of this leader/teacher concept, says Tichy, is that to be a good teacher, you have to be a good learner. As Michael Dell said, information comes in random bits, so in order to teach the valuable lessons that can be found in that information, a teacher must first collect that information and draw out those valuable lessons. Tichy calls this having a "teachable point of view." It is not enough to have knowledge and experience, "leaders must draw appropriate lessons from their experience, and then take their tacit knowledge and make it explicit to others." They must learn it for themselves before they can teach it to others.

LEARN FROM EVERYBODY

There is a natural tendency to think that the people above us on the organization chart know more than we do. So we look to them for information and guidance. (There's also the fact that they are our bosses.) But it is a real unforced error not to seek information from people throughout the organization, including at the bottom.

You'd be amazed by what you can find out if you simply ask people who work for you what you can do to make their jobs easier. They will tell you about all sorts of bottlenecks, delays, and unnecessary steps that you knew nothing about. Often a very simple fix can eliminate a nagging problem and boost both productivity and morale.

The thing to remember is that you need to make sure that you are learning from the people who are most likely to have the information that you need. If you want to know what customers are saying, one place to start is to ask the people in your organization who are talking to the customers. Salespeople have lots of valuable information, even though they are often, especially in retail businesses, part-time hourly workers. Similarly, service techs who go out to customers' offices to maintain equipment are usually toward the bottom of the organization chart, but they know a lot about your customers. So you make a big mistake if you do not learn from them.

The eyes and brains of your workers are valuable resources. It is a good idea to go out and talk to customers yourself so that you can learn from them directly, but don't forget to talk to your own people as well. You may be a manager, but they are out there on the ground all the time, so they are more tuned in to the issues that matter. When you go out into the field, you are just dropping in as the interested tourist. Your local guides who are in the area all the time can help you understand what you see.

Learn from everything. If your employer offers a class or training program that is relevant to your work, go to it. If you have the time, take a business course at the local college or in a long-distance program at a university. You can learn a lot in these classroom settings. But if you have a learning mind-set, learning won't be something you have to find time for. It will be something that happens as you go through your days with open eyes and an open mind.

ACES!

- *Make a conscious decision to learn and grow:* It all starts with a commitment to learn. This means changing your behavior by attending any in-house courses, professional training seminars, et cetera. But also look to learn from those around you, regardless of their position on the company organization chart.
- *Learn why things happen:* That was the advice of Michael Dell, who also added, "Information in its raw form doesn't present itself in neat and tidy packages." In order to make sure that you don't make an unforced error, you need a complete picture of things most relevant to your business. It is not enough to master only one or two dimensions; you need a three-dimensional picture of customers, products, employees, and so on.
- *Be a teacher and a learner:* As Noel Tichy taught us, there is a

great advantage to being both a teacher and a learner. Having a "teachable point of view" means learning something before you can teach it. The key is making sure that you are gaining the knowledge you need in order to do your job more effectively. It is also critical for you to draw out the appropriate lessons so that you can pass on what you have learned to the rest of the team or unit.

CHAPTER 10

Not Practicing Enough

Why Preparation Looms So Large

I have to give Lendl credit. Nobody in the sport has ever worked as
hard as he did. . . . Ivan wasn't the most talented player, but his
dedication—physical and mental—was incredible, second to none. . . .
And he did it all through sheer rehearsal.

—John McEnroe, in his book *You Cannot Be Serious*

John McEnroe wasn't the only one to notice how hard Ivan Lendl worked to become a number-one ranked tennis player, but he explained Lendl's success the best: "Through some difficult times, Lendl turned himself into an incredibly tough player, mentally as well as physically. He just said, 'I am going to do it until I get it right, and I'm going to keep doing it and doing it, for hours and hours and years and years.' You have to credit that type of perseverance: Very few people can stick with it that long."

Lendl became one of the best tennis players ever through sheer effort. He worked hard to stay at the top of his game. *Tennis Magazine* named him one of the ten greatest players since 1966, labeling him "the game's greatest overachiever."

The results speak volumes. Ivan Lendl won more Grand Slam singles titles than anyone in history (nineteen). And despite incredible opponents such as Jimmy Connors, Björn Borg, and John McEnroe, he dominated the sport throughout the late 1980s, breaking the record for holding the number-one spot for 270 weeks, or more than five years (only Pete Sampras bettered that record). He did it by bringing a new style of all-court power tennis to the game that he felt important enough to devote an entire book to—calling it *Hitting Hot*.

Lendl showed that preparation can make all the difference. He made sure that he was more mentally and physically prepared than his opponent, thereby making fewer unforced errors and winning more matches. McEnroe believes that today's tennis greats, male and female, are "the direct result of Lendl's example."

After beating Lendl, Pete Sampras said: "You know what the name Lendl means to me? Dedication, hard work, overcoming everybody although maybe he didn't have the tennis talent of a lot of guys. I admire him immensely."

Being prepared counts for a lot in business as well as on the tennis court. And it is something that is entirely within your control. Being prepared doesn't mean obsessing over every possible eventuality. Lightning does sometimes strike. Things are going to happen seemingly out of nowhere. If your office is in a desert, you don't want to waste your time planning for a flood (although you should have a plan for how to continue operations after a disaster.) Rather, being prepared means knowing what is going on in the areas relevant to your work and staying on top of things.

If you go to a meeting and your boss asks you about a project you are working on, can you give him up-to-date accurate information? Do you know when the work is due? Will it be done on time, or perhaps ahead of schedule? If there are problems, what are they? And can you say how you are resolving them?

You never know when you will be called on to deliver an informal or formal "presentation" on a project, an account, or an entire business. And how well you respond will affect both your reputation and your performance. Your reputation and your performance are both important. They are related, but they aren't the same thing. Your reputation reflects what people think of you. Your performance is the actual results that you deliver for the company.

For example, having good information, and having it on the tip of your tongue to share with others when they need it, will boost your reputation. People will come to see you as a reliable and competent colleague. Even the ones whose work doesn't directly rely on the information you provide will form an opinion. They will be favorably impressed if they hear you respond to questions promptly and well. They will come to think of you as a "go-to" person, as someone they can depend on when they need something from your department. But if you stumble and come across as clueless, they won't respect you. And without the respect of colleagues, you will have a much harder time keeping your job and getting ahead.

Remember, though, that your quick smooth answers must be correct. This is where the preparation comes in. If you stay on top of things and know what is going on in your territory, you will be able to answer most questions. But when you don't have a specific piece of data, it is better to say, "I'm not sure. Let me find out and get back to you," than to give out misinformation. Just make sure that you do find out and do get back to your boss and/or the team member promptly.

It is hard to overestimate the importance of having a good reputation, but if there is anything more important than having a good reputation, it is being a good performer. Most of the time, the two go together. People who perform well have good reputations, and the people who have good reputations also perform well.

But having one doesn't guarantee the other, so you have to work on both of them. I'll talk more about maintaining your reputation in another chapter (chapter 12). Here I'll just point out that if you are a good schmoozer, and you smile a lot, it will take people a lot longer to realize that you aren't performing any valuable service or delivering any valuable goods. But eventually, they will notice, and when that happens, you will be in much worse shape than you would have been if you had invested your time in learning and doing your job instead of apple polishing. On the other hand, if you do your job brilliantly, but you are withdrawn, curt, or rude, or you have a reputation for not helping your team, you will have a lot harder time being appreciated and promoted for your work. So you need to tend to both your reputation and your performance.

Now back to being prepared. It is easy to see how being prepared allows you to answer someone's questions or deliver a timely, well-documented report. Less obvious, but just as important, are some of the ways that being prepared helps you to do your job.

One of the biggest mistakes that managers make is falling into what I call "crisis-management mode." In a technology-driven world, this is especially easy to do. We are constantly accessible to anyone who knows any of our myriad electronic addresses. This means that we are bombarded with messages and new information that seem to demand responses. We feel like we never have time to step back or to look ahead because we are always dealing with some crisis. And it is more likely to be someone else's crisis than your own. This is a very dangerous way to operate.

What this essentially means is that you are letting other people decide for you what is important and to set your priorities. You are letting the last person who fired off a text message to you to hijack your attention, regardless of the merits of what's in the message as compared with what you would be doing if you weren't reading and responding to the message. When you respond equally to every stimulus, you fall into the trap of letting the urgent drive out the important.

This is "leading with your in-box," rather than "leading with your out-box." In an earlier book of mine I discussed the importance of leading with your out-box. That means taking control of your destiny and controlling your priorities. When you allow your in-box (whether it be a real one, a voice-mail system, or an e-mail in-box) to control the agenda, you are endangering your future by giving others the keys to your agenda. That's never a good idea. The most effective people lead with their out-box and do not allow other people's crises to control things.

When this happens you are not only turning every new data point into a minicrisis that needs a response, but more importantly, you are ignoring all the other things that need your attention. Eventually, these things that you could have planned for in advance show up as full-blown crises themselves. And they are crises of your own making because they didn't have to be crises. They wouldn't have been crises if you had stayed on top of the situation and been prepared.

You know, for example, that you need to get a big project out the door by a certain date. That delivery date was set several weeks ago when you made the original deal with the client or commitment to your boss. At the time, it might have been a fairly tight deadline, or it could have been a relaxed one, but it was one that you had the time to make. But in the weeks since then, you have let it sit on the back burner because you and your team were too busy dealing with "crises" and putting out other fires. Now the delivery date is only a couple of weeks away, and this project, which was a challenging but doable one, has become a crisis.

So now you push the panic button and send, or keep, your team in crisis mode. You will probably meet the deadline and come up with something, but it is very likely not as good a product as you would have had if you had worked on it at a steady, thoughtful pace.

Worse, as a manager, you are abusing and wearing out yourself and your employees. As a friend and former newspaper editor put it to me recently: "Way too often, people manage by crisis. They don't worry about, or even look at anything, until it bites them. Then they have to scramble furiously and, worse, make all their team players scramble furiously."

She went on to explain: "I was as willing as anybody to go all out and do whatever was necessary when something unexpected happened. The newspaper business is unpredictable, and I am fine with that. But what I am not fine with is a train that is coming down the track. We can all see it. We even know more or less when it is going to arrive, but everyone waits and does nothing until the rush of wind hits them in the face and then it's an all-out all-hands-on-deck panic. And heaven forbid that a real, unexpected crisis comes along at the same time. It's one of the reasons I don't work for companies anymore."

This raises another important point about being prepared: If you are prepared and on top of the things you can anticipate, when something totally surprising does happen, you will be in a much better position to mount an effective response.

THE MOST PREPARED TENNIS COACH
ON THE PLANET

Tennis professional–turned coach Brad Gilbert, whom I mentioned in the introduction of this book, is a fanatic on the subject of preparation. He thinks games are often won before the players take the court. Part 1 of his best-selling book was called "The Winning Edge: The Match Begins Before the Match Begins."

The same is true in business.

Being prepared may not make you a superstar, but it will make you a grade-A consistent player. It will make you a winner. What follows are some ideas to help you to be prepared.

ACES!

• *Find out how you best learn:* As Peter Drucker pointed out, some people learn best when they hear things, others when they see them in writing. I learn best by rewriting whatever it is that I am trying to master. Learn how you best learn so that you will be able to take in the important things you need to know and retain them. Remember Lendl: He did it by sheer rehearsal.

- *Develop a learning pattern that works for you:* Once you know how you learn, make sure that you take the time to learn. Develop a routine. If you look over your department's numbers and schedule every day, it doesn't have to take much time. You can do it at night, or you can do it in the morning. But set aside a time to do it regularly. Tennis players know almost by instinct where the lines are because they are so familiar with the territory. This preparation allows them to keep their eyes firmly focused on the ball.

- *Get familiar with every aspect of your project:* Most projects today—whether it be preparing a manuscript for publication, drafting an architectural design for a shopping center, or evaluating a company for acquisition—involve many moving parts. Of course, they differ greatly depending on the project. But make sure that you look at it from three dimensions, and all points of view. You don't want to take a chance that you will make an unforced error by missing a tough question that you did not think of because of a limited view of the project.

- *Keep control of your agenda:* Don't let every e-mail and instant message divert your attention. If you respond to each little issue that someone else brings to your attention, you will get mired in the details of what is happening now and you won't be able to look ahead and prepare yourself for what is coming. Good leaders are able to manage their departments through crises, but better managers know how to avoid them. One way they do this is by always looking ahead and preparing for what they see.

CHAPTER 11

Not Improving Your Game

Why Experimentation Is a Prerequisite to Success

Progress and improvement do not come in big bunches,
they come in little pieces.

—Arthur Ashe

Celebrated tennis writer W. Timothy Gallwey once said, "Perfect strokes are already in us, waiting to be discovered."

In business, a perfect stroke might be a sales pitch that wins a million-dollar contract, or a strategy presentation that helps you to nab that promotion you have wanted for years.

We all have "perfect strokes" within us, but in many cases we will have to try a variety of options to bring them out of us. Billie Jean King, who won a stunning thirty-nine Grand Slam titles in singles, doubles, and mixed doubles, once said, "Champions keep playing until they get it right."

The same is true of the best in business as well. The most effective managers understand that experimentation is one of the keys to success and yet another important way to reduce unforced errors.

"Getting it right" seldom happens overnight, especially when it comes to things like complex presentations, complicated product introductions, and executing on lengthy marketing plans. You have to be willing to try new things, to make mistakes, and then to try again. The best road to "perfect strokes" is through trial and error.

Children know this. They fall off their bikes and get right back up and try again. But as adults, we are too self-conscious. We don't like to be seen failing at something, so we shy away from trying anything that we don't think is a sure bet. And in the process, we lose out on the opportunity to learn and improve our game.

WE EXPERIMENT EARLY

As the father of twin, five-year-old boys I can vouch that children love to experiment. Infants "experiment" with just about anything that they can get their hands on. Toddlers, who are more mobile, explore and experiment further afield, with blocks and art projects and all kinds of things they find around the house. After all, how else can you find out if that bean will fit into your ear if you don't try it? It's in kids' DNA to try new things. Young children are naturals in this regard, and it continues until they cross over into their teens.

As adults, we think of teenagers as rebelling because they resist just about anything an adult says. But the reality is that the teenage years are a lot about learning how to conform. Adolescents can be merciless to anyone who stands out as the slightest bit unusual. So teenagers try very hard to be just like their friends.

The narrowing process continues in college as we choose a major field of study and concentrate our energies on it to the exclusion of other interests. By the time we get our first job, our desire to experiment has been greatly diminished, and we want desperately to fit in and not make waves.

All of this has the effect of making us less likely to come up with some great new idea or breakthrough in the first part of our careers. Why chance a big idea that might make us appear to be different from our peers? Worse, what if we make a bold decision and it turns out badly? It used to be said that one of the reasons that IBM was successful for so long after it had slipped out of the forefront in computer technology was that it was a "safe" choice. Even if the IBM machines weren't the best for the job, the person charged with spending a company's huge IT budget could never be blamed for buying the reliability of the IBM name.

Ironically, proposing new ideas and concepts is what gives us the best chance to set ourselves apart from the pack and get promoted. Seasoned, experienced managers understand this. They know that experimentation is key to success for both individuals and companies. People who experiment, who routinely test new ideas and concepts, are less likely to commit unforced errors because they will have experienced more possibilities and have a better knowledge of how things work. They have more tools in their tool kit, and better knowledge about how to use them.

People who experiment also have, or develop, mind-sets that make them more able to embrace change. An experimenter knows that not every idea or theory is going to work out. She may think that something should be a good idea, but when she starts testing it, she knows she may discover a fatal flaw. She is looking for the flaw, and when she finds it, she accepts the need for change and adapts. People who shy away from experimentation, who only want to stick with what is known and what is old, often find change much more frightening, so they cling to ideas and behaviors long after their usefulness has waned.

If there is one business titan who has advanced the body of knowledge in the field of experimentation, it is Andrew Grove, the cofounder and former CEO of Intel. Grove, who also won honors as *Time* magazine's 1997 Man of the Year for his development and global distribution of the microchip, is the business practitioner who perhaps most famously embraced experimentation and change.

A quick bit of history: In the mid-1980s Intel's core product, memory chips, was under fire from higher-quality, lower-priced chips from Japanese competitors. At first, managers at Intel made the unforced error warned against in chapter 1 of this book: They deluded themselves into thinking that the data they were receiving about the superiority of the Japanese chips was a mistake. But the time came when they realized that it was they who were wrong—not the data.

Eventually, the company came face-to-face with its own mortality. The first thing Grove, who was president of Intel at the time, and CEO Gordon Moore had to do was to accept the fact they needed to dramatically change course.

Even after they fully understood the problem, says Grove, they delayed. "With all the rhetoric about how management is about change, the fact is that we managers loathe change, especially when it involves us." And, in this case, Grove wasn't faced with a run-of-the-mill change. He needed to completely break with the company's past, even though it had been wildly successful, and find a new line of business.

Finally, in 1985, Grove and Moore were in Grove's office one day. Grove recalls staring out the window for a while and then saying to Moore: "If we got kicked out and the board brought in a new CEO, what do you think he would do?" Moore responded immediately, "He'd probably get us out of memories." Grove reflected for a moment. And then he said, "Why shouldn't you and I walk out the door, come back and do it ourselves?" Which is exactly what they did. Intel abandoned the memory chip business to its competitors (mostly Japanese at that point) and transformed itself into the world's leading maker of micro-processors.

Grove, an engineer, and Moore, a scientist, had the advantage of being comfortable with experimentation. This helped them take the bold step that allowed them to become the masters of Intel's transformation instead of the "victims" of a global shift in the market.

The Intel story brings me to another important reason that experimentation is a key to success. It is that experimentation gives you options. When Intel needed to abandon the memory chip business, it had already been exploring microprocessors. It had a Plan B waiting in the wings when Plan A went off the tracks.

If managers and employees are consistently experimenting with new products and processes, they may be able to make the minor adjustments necessary to stay ahead of the market. They might be able to avoid undergoing the kind of gut-wrenching change described here. But that's something you can't count on because the fate of your unit, team, or company is never totally in your control. New competitors can come along (as in Intel's case), or a new technology can turn the landscape upside down (like what happened to the Sony Walkman when iPod was born), or the economy can go to hell, taking your management team down a path it could never have imagined.

"Resolution of strategic dissonance does not come in the form of a figurative light bulb going on," asserts Grove. "It comes through experimentation." As a leader on a corporate level, Grove suggests that you should encourage experimentation by loosening up "the level of control that your organization normally is accustomed to. Let people try different techniques, review different products, exploit different sales channels and go after different customers. . . . Only stepping out of the old ruts will bring new insights."

One of the realities, Grove points out, is that you cannot simply turn on and off an experimentation switch whenever it is convenient. "The dilemma is that you can't suddenly start experimenting when you realize you're in trouble, unless you've been experimenting all along. . . . Ideally, you should have experimented with new products, technologies, channels, promotions, and new customers all along. Then, when you sense that 'something has changed,' you will have a number of experiments that can be relied on to expand your bag of tricks and your organization will be in a much better position."

GOOGLE: EXPERIMENTATION AT ITS CORE

Google is another company whose habits and practices are geared toward experimentation. The company founders Larry Page and Sergey Brin, for example, insist that its engineers take one day a week to work on their own favorite projects. Google also has an "ideas mailing" in which anyone with a new idea can add it to the list (but then must vigorously defend the idea when presenting it to management).

Nikesh Arora, president of European, Middle Eastern, and African markets and a senior VP of Google, told an interviewer: "The real engine of Google's success is its innovation. Consequently, we look to our managers to encourage innovation and guide it to scale, so that it can make a global impact. Google's success has been built squarely on the shoulders of our amazing employees. Google has done well because we've provided a great work environment where people can literally change the world. As Google grows, we're still committed to this culture that fosters rapid innovation."

Jonathan Rosenberg is a Google executive VP who leads the company's innovation efforts. Rosenberg cites Peter Drucker when imparting advice on how to select and retain the most talented knowledge workers. In an official company blog, Rosenberg says that the company looks for people with "non-routine problem solving skills" and cites five ways to find these "non-traditional savants." These include searching for people who possess analytical reasoning abilities, strong communication skills, and a willingness to experiment. "It's easy to educate for the routine, and hard to educate for the novel," explains Rosenberg.

Why does Google search out people with a penchant for experimentation? "Non-routine problems call for non-routine solutions and there is no formula for success," asserts Rosenberg. "A well-designed experiment calls for a range of treatments, explicit control groups, and careful post-treatment analysis. Sometimes an experiment kills off a pet theory, so you need a willingness to accept the evidence even if you don't like it."

Companies such as Google that are highly dependent on innovation think a lot about how to encourage and make the most of experimentation. One Google concept promoted by Marissa Mayer, VP of search products and user experience, is particularly important and original:

"Don't ditch projects—morph them." The idea here is about building on experimentation. If you try something and it doesn't work out as you hoped, don't abandon the experiment: Redirect it. Take what you have learned and apply it to something that may turn out to be more productive.

One of the ironies about experimentation is that people who are experimenters never expect perfection, yet they are the ones who get closest to it. They know, like Arthur Ashe did, that "Progress and improvement do not come in big bunches, they come in little pieces." So they are willing to take calculated risks. They are willing to think outside the box, and to actually step outside the box to try untested things. And their success is due, in no small part, to their attitude. When they try an experiment and it fails, they don't see failure, they see an opportunity to try again, with a better base of knowledge to build on.

ACES!

- *Don't lose the urge to experiment:* Rather than simply trying to fit in, come to terms with the reality that the managers and organizations that practice experimentation on a consistent basis come out on top the most often. Fight the impulse to be a "conformist" as you get older.
- *Expect change:* This is a lesson taught to us by Intel cofounder Andy Grove. Be mentally prepared to walk away from the past. And anticipate the future by experimenting, so when you need a new option, you will have some available.
- *Take a page from Google and don't wait for perfection before putting ideas into action:* At Google they launch new site features in small beta experiments before going national. They do not wait for perfection but instead move quickly and improve as they go. If you can do the equivalent in your business you will fend off unforced operating errors by being a first or early mover.

CHAPTER 12

Not Watching the Whole Court

How to Protect Your Flanks

However good your shots, however fast your movement and reflexes,
all is lost if the mind is not controlling every move.

—Ken Rosewall, eight-time Grand Slam singles winner. From
the 1975 book, *Play Tennis with Rosewall: The Little Master
and His Method*

Eight-time Grand Slam winner Ken Rosewall was a superb shot maker, but in his eyes, being the best shot maker wasn't what made him a winner. What made him a winner was that he was in command of the court. He paid attention to what was going on everywhere around him and responded to all threats.

Off the court, in the world of business, being the best often isn't enough to make you a winner, either. Being the best certainly helps, but other things matter, too.

This chapter is about corporate maneuvering. Some people call it "office politics." I don't like that term because I think it suggests that they are frivolous and unimportant. Call it what you will. I am talking here about the interpersonal, nonperformance-related factors that inevitably will affect how well you succeed in your career.

Career expert Dr. Kathleen Reardon puts it like this: "To the successful executive in a competitive organization, day-to-day life is politics. There is no doubt that a high level of field-based competence is needed to get ahead. But choose any two competent people, and the one who has political savvy, agility in the use of power, and the ability to influence others will go further."

You do not need to be an executive or even a manager for your career to be affected by the turf wars and power plays that take place every day in your office. They are part of the environment in every office. So this chapter will help you to make sure that you do not get fatally wounded by some backstabbing colleague. It will also suggest some positive political steps you can take that will help your career. What it will not do is counsel you on how to wield your dagger to kill off your rivals. Remember, the way to get ahead is to avoid making unforced errors and not to worry about how well, or badly, your peers are doing.

Regarding office politics, my basic advice is to avoid them whenever possible. I have had a very good career engaging in them very little. However, avoiding them is not the same as ignoring them. You avoid poisonous snakes but you don't ignore them. Even though you don't want to engage in office politics, you do need to be always keenly aware of them. And when you sense a danger, you must act swiftly and effectively. It's unfortunate that you have to do this, but it is part of the reality of going to work in a corporation where many people interact every day.

Throughout the years I have always been very mindful of where I stand in the eyes of my bosses and what my peers are saying about me. It doesn't mean that I spend time playing games, gossiping about my peers, or calculating my next promotion. In fact, those are the sorts of behaviors that can divert your attention from doing your job well, and will cause you to make unforced error after unforced error. Nonetheless, you do need to pay attention to politics and watch your flanks.

KEEP YOUR EYE ON THE BALL

Your biggest responsibility in any organization or corporation is to do a great job by blowing away the goals that have been assigned to you. This means that you need to use all of your time wisely, allowing for as few distractions as possible. Of course, there are always things that are going to eat into your time—from getting coffee, to chatting with colleagues, to going out to lunch. But you need to minimize these activities, especially those that take you away from performing the tasks that actually add value to your firm.

One way to manage your time is to make sure you come to work every day with a firm idea or plan of exactly what it is you want to accomplish that day. I have made a habit of jotting down my top two to three priorities either the night before, just before quitting time, or in the early morning, before starting my day (I typically begin at 5:00 a.m. because I am a morning person, and do my best editing then).

I usually have several priorities on my list, but I always have one overriding priority that takes center stage every day. In my line of work, it may be finding the ideal author for a particular project, or editing a book that is due to production at the end of the week.

This discussion about setting priorities may seem like a diversion from the theme here of dealing with office politics. But one of the best ways to stay focused on your priorities is to have a clear view every morning of what those priorities for this particular day are. This will help make you much less likely to get bogged down in distractions, like petty, office politicking.

Even though it should be your general policy to disdain politicking and jockeying for position in the office hierarchy, there are occasions when you do need to venture at least into the neighborhood of politics. For example, when you discover that someone is putting out false or misleading information that is hurting your reputation, you must respond immediately, not by tearing down the person you feel is misrepresenting you, but by setting the record straight.

A friend of mine, the newspaper editor I mentioned earlier, says that one of the biggest unforced errors she ever made was not responding when she knew that others were complaining about her. "I was the editor who decided what stories ran in the paper and where they ran. A couple of the bureau chiefs whose reporters would send in stories used to complain whenever I didn't run their stories as prominently or as long as they wanted. They even told me that they were complaining to my boss, but I thought they were just being whiners. I had to evaluate the importance of all the stories I received each day from all of the reporters in all of the bureaus, and I was confident that I was making good decisions. Further, I never heard any complaints from my boss. So I decided that I wasn't going to go running to him like a crybaby just because these bureau chiefs were." Only months later, she says, when she was "promoted" to a less responsible staff job, did she hear from her boss, "Well, you know there have been a lot of complaints about you." When she asked, he never said that he himself was unhappy with her decisions. The only two people he mentioned were the two who had been complaining to her. There apparently were many others who weren't complaining and even saying nice things, but these two, because they were so persistent, had succeeded in coloring his opinion. "Lesson number one," she now says, "Protect your flanks. Make sure that you get your side of the story to the judge."

This brings me to the next important point. Make sure that you know who the judge is. On the tennis court, you know the judge is the person sitting in the high chair at the side of the court. You can see her right there watching you. It's far murkier in the working world.

Often your boss is the judge, the key person who decides if you are doing a good job and deserve a raise or a promotion. But that is not always the case.

Take a step back and get an even broader view of the whole court. It may be that your boss is ineffective, and has no real power or ability to make a decision. That could be because your boss is simply clueless, someone who got promoted because of his technical knowledge, not his managerial know-how. Or it could be that his boss is a micromanager, using your boss as a puppet.

The key is to figure out who the real decider is, and to do that, you need to figure out who holds the greatest sway over your boss. In several of the companies I worked for, my boss's boss was the one who made the greatest decisions affecting my life—and the life of my direct reports. And often you do not figure this out until something happens, some event that causes your boss to rush the net, so to speak, where you can see his entire game up close and personal.

Here is an example: I was the middle manager responsible for a group of people who did what I did; they published books. My boss regarded one of my editors as a lightweight, someone who simply didn't get it. My boss was even angry that this guy—let's call him Bob—was still on the staff. But when this "uninformed" individual received a job offer from our biggest competitor, my boss's boss, who had a far more favorable view of Bob, stepped in. My boss's boss insisted that we not only keep him, but offer Bob a near-unprecedented 20-plus percent raise—far more than what the competitor was offering.

In this situation, for this particular employee, it didn't matter what his boss thought or what his boss's boss thought. It was Bob's boss's boss's boss that pulled all of the strings! I suspect that is the case in many companies today. Senior managers give great lip service to empowerment and then make sure that no one but them makes all the important decisions.

That is why you need to have a wide view of the entire court. Otherwise, you may find yourself—and your future—in the hands of

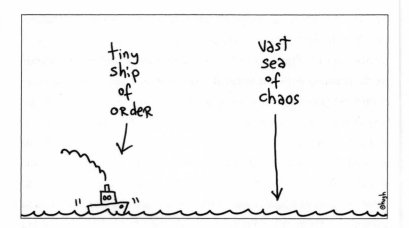

people you almost never see or interact with, and that's a definite setup for an unforced error.

LOOK PAST THE ORG CHART

In the case I described above, the "decider" was a manager who was "stacked" on top of others on the org chart. However, organizational life is seldom that clear-cut.

Your boss may indeed be the one who decides your fate, but he may be listening to other people. Remember the case of my friend the newspaper editor. Her boss was listening to and influenced by his other direct reports.

But there may be other people out there who have influence. For example, your boss may seek the opinions of people in your department who work for you or people in administrative positions who have to deal with you. Or maybe there is someone three departments removed from you who has no firsthand knowledge of your work, but she hangs out at the water cooler and also rides the same commuter train with your boss. She fills his ear with gossip on the way to work each morning.

I have personally seen and heard of careers ruined because of a boss's tendency to listen to one person among many vying for his or her attention. In the most noxious case of this and also the most extreme, I worked for a boss who listened to one person because that person brought in a lot of business. That was my boss's unforced error, and a significant one. Just because an individual is a rainmaker, it doesn't mean he knows anything about assessing talent or helping to manage a company or unit. That's why so many managers are not fit to be in the position. They get promoted for the wrong reasons.

Even if your boss is a good, fair, thoughtful person who does her job well, you still need make sure that you protect yourself and your reputation with her. You cannot count on your good work to do all the talking. That's because all good decision makers make it a policy to listen to various points of view. And even the most independent and secure decision makers, are vulnerable to falling for misinformation, especially if that misinformation is never challenged or counteracted with good information from you.

The sad fact is that once the boss forms a negative opinion of you, it is almost impossible to get her to change her mind. That makes the nasty person in the next cubicle all the more powerful.

One more word on the subject: Never fall into the trap of trading barbs with a fellow employee or manager to a superior. That is a losing strategy. Even if it is done completely behind closed doors and that senior person promises no retribution, do not take the bait.

Let's take a specific example: What if your boss's boss asks you up to his office to find out your opinion of your boss? Even if you detest your boss, do you tell the truth? This is a thornier question because your boss's boss can be asking you this for all of the right reasons. Perhaps he heard that your boss is a bully and wants to help matters. My advice? Don't pour your heart out as the risk outweighs the potential benefit. There are too many reasons that you might be asked for this information, and one of the most prominent is to test your allegiance to the firm and its managers. Even if you despise your boss, find a way of saying something that is innocuous and cannot come back to bite you.

PROTECT YOUR FLANKS

So far I have mostly discussed opinions about your fellow managers and bosses where there are honest disagreements. These are situations in which people have different opinions based on where they sit in the organization. But unfortunately, there are many toxic work environments where people are actively gunning for each other or for a specific individual. This sort of thing can happen at any time and to anyone, even to someone with a sterling reputation.

For example, it happened to the former CEO of Ford, Jacques

Nasser, who, just a year or so earlier, was considered the golden boy of the car industry. However, when crisis hit in the form of a massive recall of the Bridgestone tires on Ford's best-selling Explorer vehicles, he was far too busy putting out fires to consider what others were whispering about him behind his back. Members of his senior management team did an end run by talking directly to William Clay Ford and poisoning the Nasser well.

By the time Nasser learned of his mistake it was too late. He was out, and William Clay Ford, the great-grandson of the founder, took over. In this case, Nasser was the CEO, but still he was vulnerable to office politics. His failure was not securing buy-in from the various constituencies affected by tough decisions he made. It is a classic case of an unforced error and can take place at every level of the company.

So if you discover that your name is being sullied, how do you prevent this scenario from engulfing your future in flames?

One of the first things you need to do is to establish a very strong working relationship with your manager. But as I said earlier, since you can't be sure who wields the most decision-making authority in your organization, you need to develop a network of people so you are not the last to know when someone is trashing you and your good name.

As a rule of thumb, I made it my business to spend time with a great variety of people in the companies I worked for, and not just those whom I knew had direct influence over my career.

This reaching out has not only prevented unforced errors, but has solidified my place in the company by consistently enhancing my

profile in a positive way. Besides, maintaining strong working relationships with people throughout the company pays all sorts of dividends that may not be readily apparent (for example, when you need
some numbers from the finance department on the spot because you
have been tapped to make a presentation to the powers that be the
very next day).

Ultimately, what you really need to do is to make sure that you
and the people who are going to judge your work and impact your
career are in sync. You need to make sure you do your job well and
that the "judges" know you are doing it well.

This leads us right into the last part of the book, the epilogue. In
this last section I explore various theories on what it means to not
only make fewer unforced errors, but to become the best at something. I will do that through the lens of books designed to help people
become expert performers in their particular fields.

ACES!

- *Avoid, but don't ignore, office politics:* It's a better to use your
  time doing a good job than trying to gain some strategic position or tearing down someone else. Nonetheless, you need to
  stay tuned in so that some other backstabber doesn't make you
  his victim. Protect your flanks.
- *Forge strategic relationships within your organization:* This
  will help you on any number of fronts and pay dividends when
  you least expect it. Reach out to people in other departments

and try to break down the walls that might have been built up over the years.

- *Find out who the real line judge is in your game:* In some situations your boss will decide your future. In others, it will be her boss or her boss's boss or someone your boss listens to. It is incumbent upon you to figure out who the real "decider" is and make sure that person knows how capable you truly are.

- *Meet with your manager on a consistent basis:* Even if it is only fifteen minutes a week, having a weekly meeting with your manager can help you to keep abreast of key company developments, changing priorities, and areas in which your boss could use your help. Find a time that is convenient for your manager and make sure that you tell your manager how grateful you are for his time. Also, try to find subtle ways to make sure that your manager knows of your latest triumphs (if, for some reason, he isn't aware of them). If you think there is a real threat to your reputation, address it directly.

- *Come to every meeting completely prepared, agenda in hand:* When meeting with your boss bring with you a list of a few key priorities that you want to discuss (listed in order of importance). I had an employee who I felt was totally disorganized except for that one time each week when he brought a short list of items that he wanted to go over with me. It helped him to boost his standing with me and to protect his flanks.

Beyond the Unforced Error

For Expert-Level Performance, Keep at It

> *It takes five years to make a tennis player,*
> *and ten years to make a champion.*
> —Bill Tilden, from his 1925 instructional book, *Match Play*
> *and the Spin of the Ball*

Bill Tilden was a star tennis player and major celebrity of the 1920s. He won about a dozen Grand Slam singles events and was ranked number one in the world for seven straight years.

But for all his victories, Tilden was not an overly talented tennis player. Rather, like Ivan Lendl sixty years later, he was a man who worked very hard at his craft. Tilden was not the number one player at his high school and he didn't even make the tennis team at the University of Pennsylvania. But after he dropped out of college, he dedicated himself to improving his game. And like Lendl, he came to dominate the sport.

"I am a great believer in practice, but above all in intensive practice," wrote Tilden in his 1925 book. "My idea of intensive practice is to pick out one stroke and hammer away at that shot until it is completely mastered."

Most star athletes know the importance and value of hard work. Althea Gibson once said: "Most of us who aspire to be tops in our field don't really consider the amount of work required to stay tops." Ms. Gibson, the daughter of sharecroppers who came from the hardscrabble streets of Harlem, won eleven major tennis titles in the 1950s and in 1957 was the first African American to garner the "Female Athlete of the Year" award. She won again in 1958.

Everyone knows that star tennis players practice for hours, days, and years. To play tennis at the highest level—to be ranked among the world's best players—requires an incredible commitment and almost always starting at an early age. But it is not just true for tennis.

Bill Tilden was a methodical person who practiced hard and he also thought a lot about how to become a winner. He wrote multiple books on the subject. And his conclusion that it takes ten years of intensive practice to make a champion was a forerunner of current thinking on how people become expert-level performers in business as well.

THE REWARDS OF BEING THE BEST

For most of this book, I have covered how you can be a winner simply by making the fewest unforced errors. I have talked about how to play a steady, consistent, winning game. And it is true that you don't have to be the strongest player to outlast your competitors. But it doesn't hurt to be an ace (and besides it's fun.) So in closing, I want to turn to some research on the topic of how to become truly great at something. As we will see, being a world-class performer has less to do with being born with some great innate ability than it does with developing one's skills.

In all areas of life, it pays handsomely to be the best at what you do, to play at a level that makes you—for lack of a better phrase—world class. Achieving that in your work life will certainly help you to make far fewer unforced errors at whatever it is you do. And as we discussed in chapter 8, if you are viewed as world class at something, then any unforced error you make will be mitigated by the overall perception of you as a leader in your field.

But there are many more rewards for being the best. Seth Godin, best-selling author and blogger, declared in his book *The Dip*, "Being the best in the world is seriously underrated." He notes that "our culture celebrates superstars. We reward the product or the song or the organization or the employee that is number one. The rewards are heavily skewed, so much so that it's typical for #1 to get ten times the benefit of #10, and a hundred times the benefit of #100."

"Anyone who is going to hire you, buy from you, recommend you, vote for you, or do what you want them to do is going to wonder if you're the best choice."

HOW TO BECOME THE BEST

Over the centuries researchers have looked at peak performers and tried to explain why and how some people become the best. And many notable ones have come to the conclusion that in several different areas of endeavor, it takes ten years or ten thousand hours of consistent work to become an expert performer.

Two of the earliest researchers on the topic of expert performance, William Lowe Bryan and Noble Harter, wrote about this subject more than a century ago. They asserted that it took ten years for one particular type of worker—a telegrapher—to develop the expertise to be a real professional: "Our evidence is that it takes ten years to make a thoroughly seasoned press dispatcher," they stated in 1899. They also noticed that there were periods in which there was no improvement at all followed by bursts of growth.

In 1986, Charles Garfield, who led a team of scientists, engineers, and other professionals on NASA's Apollo 11 mission, published the book *Peak Performers,* based on eighteen years of research on what it takes to be an extraordinary achiever. Garfield looked at outstanding people of all shapes and sizes from corporate CEOs to a cabdriver to a toll-booth employee. He described them as "people who translate mission into results, people who are the basic unit of excellence in every organization."

Garfield said he discovered that almost anyone can gain the skills to excel, not just "rare and remote individuals who miraculously achieve far beyond the norm." He noted these peak performers "are always willing to evolve and grow, to learn from the work, as well as to complete it, to be 'better than I ever was.'" He also reiterated throughout the book that "commitment to one's work is the key source of peak performance."

More recently, authors Malcolm Gladwell and Geoff Colvin have both written books on people who achieve expert-level performance, and they have similarly concluded that excellence depends on effort and experience. It turns out that the old joke is true. The way to Carnegie Hall really is through practice, practice, practice.

Gladwell's book is called *Outliers*. Outliers, as Gladwell describes them, are people who perform at world-class levels, but he finds that they do so not because they were born with some amazing talent but because they worked at being "markedly different" from most everybody else.

There is no doubt that certain people succeed because they have better opportunities in life. Bill Gates got an early start in computers because his private junior high school had enough money to buy a computer long before most other schools. Gates was also fortunate to have been born in 1955. This is significant because it made him a teenager just at the time when modern computers began to be available. Other mid-1950s babies include: Paul Allen (cofounder, Microsoft), Steve Balmer (CEO, Microsoft), Steve Jobs (cofounder, Apple), Eric Schmidt (CEO, Google), and the three founders of Sun Microsystems, including Scott McNealy.

But opportunity is just a small part of the equation. Gladwell also cites research that shows that "excellence at performing a complex task requires a critical minimum level of practice. [It] surfaces again and again in studies of expertise. In fact, researchers have settled on what they believe is the magic number for true expertise: ten thousand hours."

One of Gladwell's most colorful examples of outliers is the Beatles. They were no instant phenomenon, Gladwell shows us. In fact, by the time they arrived in the United States in 1964, they had already performed together twelve hundred times. That's an astounding number, as most bands don't perform together twelve hundred times over their entire careers. He also pointed out that the time from their founding to their best albums—*Sgt. Pepper's Lonely Hearts Club Band* and *The Beatles* (the White Album)—was a decade.

But that wasn't the most colorful part of the story. The best part is where they performed: They went on live and played seven days a week until the early morning hours, not in hip venues such as concerts halls or rock-and-roll palladiums; no, the Beatles mastered their craft in strip clubs! As it turned out, Hamburg, Germany, did not have venues for rockers. It had strip clubs and the manager of one came up with the idea of having live bands play there all the time (it must have been good for business). Once one strip club started with bands, the rest followed suit.

And most of the bands that played in Hamburg in the late 1950s and early 1960s were from Liverpool. Without those strip clubs, the Beatles may never have been born. So by the time they got to the

United States, they were already exceptional performers with well over ten thousand hours under their belt.

Geoff Colvin asserts in his book *Talent Is Overrated* that "a number of researchers now argue that talent means nothing like what we think it means, if indeed it means anything at all." Colvin contends that it is not some born talent that translates into greatness. Instead, he says, "In studies of accomplished individuals, researchers have found few signs of precocious achievement before the individuals started intensive training." The researchers, says Colvin, think that talent may be irrelevant to greatness. And Colvin is not talking about only one field such as sports, but includes everything from music to theater, comedy, and yes, business.

As an example of the latter, he cites Jack Welch, the man that Colvin's own magazine named Manager of the Century. Colvin explains that until his mid-twenties, Welch showed no special aptitude for business because he wasn't even interested in business. He was working on his PhD in chemical engineering (earned at the University of Illinois), a far cry from business.

Both Gladwell and Colvin also cite the same researcher, K. Anders Ericsson, whose greatest contribution is the concept of "deliberate practice."

"Deliberate" or "well-structured practice," according to Ericsson, is "focused, programmatic, carried out over extended periods of time, guided by conscious performance monitoring, evaluated by analysis of level of expertise reached, identification of errors, and procedures directed at eliminating errors."

The last part of the definition shows why the concept of deliberate or well-structured practice fits into this book; it focuses on improvement over time that is monitored, as well as the "identification" and "elimination of errors."

In short, deliberate practice is hard, grueling repetitive work. In some areas, such as performing on the piano, researchers found it takes seventeen years from the performer's first formal lesson to the time she gains international recognition in the field (the fastest was twelve years). For Olympic swimmers, it took fifteen years. But ten years was the researcher's most common number for most careers or endeavors.

The practice, however, must be very specific to the field that one hopes to excel in, whether it be playing chess, playing a musical instrument, writing professionally, or playing a particular position in a particular sport, like a football receiver or quarterback.

Ericsson's description of deliberate practice does not end there: "Specific goals are set at successive stages of expertise development. It involves appropriate, immediate feedback about performance. The feedback can be obtained from objective observers—human teachers and coaches—or it can be self-generated by comparing one's own performance with examples of more advanced expert performance."

In his book, Colvin goes into rich detail about what the concept of deliberate practice means for people aiming to achieve excellence:

- *Deliberate practice means countless hours of repetition:* There was an extensive research study with music students, and Colvin explains that the music students who practiced two hours a day versus fifteen minutes a day were put in an elite group that far outdistanced the less practiced musicians. The difference is that the elite group practiced 800 percent more than the other group.

- *Deliberate practice means focusing all of your efforts on specific performance:* Citing Ericsson and his colleagues, Colvin reports on their finding that: "the difference between expert performers and normal adults reflect a life-long period of deliberate effort to improve performance in a specific domain." This dispels "the myth of the natural." To be great, you need to practice, and your practice has to be focused like a laser on improving performance in a very specific field.

- *Deliberate practice requires hard, demanding work and is not fun:* Colvin tells the story of ex-football player Jerry Rice as a textbook example of deliberate practice that worked. Rice was probably the best professional football receiver of all time. And it was common knowledge that it was because he worked harder than anyone during the football season. His sprints, running exercises, and incredible weight training were so hard that some players who tried it got sick. Yet in the off-season he repeated this regimen six days a week.

Ericsson's research showed that the ten years of deliberate practice could take many forms, including "formal education, private instruction, coaching or mentoring, exposure to domain-specific role models, and various forms of self education."

However, researchers also agree that "the specific nature of the instruction depends greatly on the type of expertise being acquired. . . . For example, outstanding leaders require different educational experiences than do exceptional creators, and, within eminent creators, distinguished scientists need distinct educational experiences than do illustrious artists."

So what you practice is just as important as how much you practice. This would explain some very compelling data that Colvin cites. According to him, many people fail to improve at their jobs regardless of the number of years they spend doing it.

This shows that experience by itself is not the issue. Colvin wrote: "In field after field, when it came to centrally important skills—stockbrokers recommending stocks, parole officers predicting recidivism, college admission officials judging applicants—people with lots of experience were no better at their jobs than those with very little experience." The key was that they needed deliberate practice and experience in the specific abilities required to do the job well.

For this reason, it is very important that at every step along the way in your career, you not only identify the skills you need to succeed, but also learn the right way to do them. Imagine spending ten years or ten thousand hours working at something, only to discover that you were practicing the wrong thing, or that you were just reinforcing a sloppy way to it.

So the good news and the bad news is that you don't need a special talent to be a world-class achiever, but you do have to work very hard at it. With deliberate practice over a ten-year period—over ten thousand hours, depending upon which theory you subscribe to—an ordinary performer can be transformed into an extraordinary one.

Expert performance comes from learning the right things to do and learning to do them right. It takes years of practice.

ACES!

- *Make up your mind to be "the best" at something:* It might be the best in your organization or industry, or the best at something in your city or town. Have confidence. You can do it. It's not about talent: It's about focus and hard work.
- *Find your passion:* The key to getting great at anything is to figure out what you love to do. You need to spend a lot of time at it, so it has to be important to you. If it isn't important to you, you probably won't put in the effort to become a star. But even if you do, think how miserable you will be not only for the ten years—or ten thousand hours—when you are climbing toward the peak, but also for the time afterward when it is still your profession.
- *Figure out what matters:* Putting in hours and years of effort won't get you there if you are not working on the things that count. Figure out what the stars in your field do differently or better than the people who are just okay. Then focus your practice on them.

- *Make a commitment:* Whatever area or profession you are in, you need to make a commitment to work at it every day or almost every day and push yourself to the limit. And you have to do it for a long time. But do not give up just because you think that you lack the skills. You can acquire the skills and attain excellence if you really want it and are willing to work for it.

ACKNOWLEDGMENTS

This book could not have been written without the support and encouragement of several key, knowledgeable players who are always selfless in their support. Together, this talented team helped to make this book a far stronger project.

The Portfolio team at Penguin is simply second to none. My mentor, boss, and editor, Adrian Zackheim, was a key supporter from the start and offered sound suggestions throughout the publishing process.

Associate editor Courtney Young offered insightful and excellent recommendations and sagacious advice, and I am once again in her debt for her wisdom and hands-on management of the project.

Nancy Cardwell, a good friend of Portfolio's and a very talented editor, made some very important edits and suggestions throughout the book—and I was very grateful to have her assistance. (Examples include the quotes she provided on pages 120 and 136.)

I have the most supportive family in the world. My wife, Nancy, and twin boys, Noah and Joshua, always gave me the time to write, even if it meant having one boy on my left arm, and the other on the right. Nancy, who edits so much of my work, was generous in helping me with this project as well. Thanks to her, certain details—such as the selection of cartoons—went off without a hitch. Nancy's final read of the work also added real value to the book. Nancy and the boys are my life, and I am truly blessed to have them.

Those cartoons are the work of Hugh McLeod, a most talented cartoonist who has made a brilliant career by creating cartoons on the back of business cards. You can view his excellent work at gapingvoid.com, a site I highly recommend.

Lastly, I thank my parents, Trudy and Barton, and my brother, Paul, who always encouraged me and offered career-enhancing advice for many years.

It is no accident that this book is dedicated to my mother. It was she who not only encouraged me, but played a role in the preparation of so many papers—going all the way back to Bronx Science. Through my family's unending assistance, they transformed an ordinary apartment in the Bronx into a learning organization all its own.

The majority of the first-person stories that appear in this book are actual events that took place over my twenty-eight-year career in business (not counting my precollege years working in my father's butcher shop and in a Bronx liquor store). In some instances I have changed the gender of the person to make sure that these people remain anonymous.

There were many sources that played a prominent role in helping me with the research phase of this book. Zenger and Folkman's *The Extraordinary Leader*, which argues for the enhancement of strengths over the fixing of weaknesses as a way to reduce unforced errors and use strengths to advance your career, was a great help in crafting Chapter 8.

Two books that were instrumental in the writing of the epilogue were Malcolm Gladwell's *Outliers* and Geoff Colvin's *Talent Is Overrated.*

The majority of the tennis quotes that appear at the beginning of each chapter are excerpted from three books: Paul Fein's *You Can Quote Me on That,* Fein's *Tennis Confidential,* and Criswell Freeman's *The Tennis Lover's Book of Wisdom.*

What follows are the individual source notes that correspond with the quotes that appear in the book, chapter by chapter, cited by page number.

Introduction: Unforced Errors: The Great Career Killers

1 "There are great visionaries who accomplish little": Larry Bossidy and Del Jones, "CEOs Take a Lesson from Tennis," *USA Today,* July 2, 2004, Money Section, p. 1.

3 McEnroe was so outraged with the loss that he vowed to stay off the court for six months: John McEnroe, *You Cannot Be Serious* (New York: Putnam, 2002), p. 222.

5 The statistic of CEO turnover up nearly 60 percent from 1995 to 2006 came from Jamie Corsi, CNBC.com, May 22, 2007, and the newsletter *Dealbreaker,* May 22, 2007.

5 Roberto Goizueta taking the company from $4 billion to $145 billion: *Wall Street Journal,* October 20, 1997, p. 1. Also in Mike Cheatham, *Your Friendly Neighborhood* (Macon, Georgia: Mercer Press, 1999), p. 2.

6 "Today's wow idea can be tomorrow's failure": Umesh Ramakrishnan, *There's No Elevator to the Top* (New York: Portfolio, 2008), p. 7.

6   Brian Sullivan's estimate of CEO tenure to be "between five and six years," Ibid, p. 7.

Chapter 1: The Ball Was Out by a Mile

16   "I think self-awareness is probably the most important thing": Billie Jean King, quoted in Paul Fein, *You Can Quote Me on That* (Dulles, Virginia: Potomac Books, 2005), p. 30.

17   "It's a big challenge, because the agenda is always shifting": Sir John Browne, *The Mind of the CEO* (New York: Basic Books, 2001), p. 149.

18   "Success always makes obsolete the very behavior that achieved it": Peter Drucker, *The Essential Drucker* (New York: Collins Business, 2008), p. 26.

22   "drifts steadily away from realism": Larry Bossidy and Ram Charan, *Confronting Reality* (New York: Crown Books, 2004).

22   "Many people in business today are boxed in": Ibid.

22   The three questions beginning with: "What's the nature of the game [business] we are in?": Ibid, p. 11.

Chapter 2: Choosing the Wrong Partner

29   "If you remember only one thing": Harry Hopman, quoted in Paul Fein, *You Can Quote Me on That* (Dulles, Virginia: Potomac Books, 2005), p. 175.

30 "If we didn't spend four hours on placing a man": Peter Drucker, *Adventures of a Bystander* (New York: Wiley, 1998), pp. 280–81.

31 The discussion of people, strategy, and crisis calls and the discussion of "emotional attachments" are found in Noel Tichy and Warren Bennis, *Judgment* (New York: Portfolio, 2008), p. 24.

35 "Whether Franklin D. Roosevelt was a great President or a national disaster has been argued hotly": Peter F. Drucker, *The Practice of Management* (New York: Harper & Row, 1954), p. 9.

36 The discussion of the importance of people and the quote: "The good-to-great leaders understood three important truths," is excerpted from Jim Collins, *Good to Great* (New York: Collins, 2001), p. 42.

36 "Second, if you have the right people on the bus": Ibid.

36 "Third, with the wrong people, it doesn't matter": Ibid.

Chapter 3: Sticking with the Wrong Partner

40 "Never change a winning game": Bill Tilden, quoted in Criswell Freeman, ed., *The Tennis Lover's Book of Wisdom* (Nashville, Tennessee: Walnut Grove Press, 1997), p. 104.

41 "failing to fix people problems in time" and other findings about CEO failure, Ram Charan and Geoff Colvin, "Why CEOs Fail," *Fortune Magazine,* June 21, 1999, p. 70.

47 Schoonover called many of the company's ills "self-induced," *New York Post,* December 27, 2007.

Chapter 4: Overlooking the Wild Card

50 "Champions are people who want to leave their sport better off": Arthur Ashe, quoted in Paul Fein, *You Can Quote Me on That* (Dulles, Virginia: Potomac Books, 2005), p. 23.

55 "Right after talent, health and conditioning, confidence is about the most important thing a tennis player can possess": James Blake, *Breaking Back* (New York: HarperCollins, 2007), p. 13.

Chapter 5: Not Keeping Your Game Inbounds

59 "For the first few years, I almost never spoke an obscenity to an umpire": John McEnroe, *You Cannot Be Serious* (New York: Putnam, 2002), p. 91.

64 The GE Values that appear in this chapter—"GE Leaders. . . Always with Unyielding Integrity"—are excerpted from the "Shared Values" that Jack Welch and a team of consultants wrote in the mid-1980s at Crotonville. They appeared in several books, including the paperback cover of Robert Slater's *The GE Way Fieldbook* (New York: McGraw-Hill, 2000).

65 "The only thing that works is management by values": *Inside Steve's Brain* (New York: Portfolio, 2007).

65 "find people who are competent and really bright": Ibid.

Chapter 6: Always Playing with a Singles Mind-set

70 "No matter what accomplishments you make": Althea Gibson, quoted in Paul Fein, *You Can Quote Me on That* (Dulles, Virginia: Potomac Books, 2005), p. 28.

74 "I always loved doubles. I love playing on teams": Martina Navratilova, quoted in *You Can Quote Me on That*, p. 172.

74 "conducts and orchestrates a system": Chris Conde, Steve Tappin, and Andrew Cave, *The Secrets of CEOs* (London: Nicholas Brealey Publishing, 2008), p. 218.

74 "It is very arrogant to think you can make better decisions": Ibid.

74 "The role of the boss is to make a handful of decisions": Ibid.

Chapter 7: Not Stepping Up to the Net

82 "I must keep a strict command over myself": Charlotte "Lottie" Dodd, quoted in Paul Fein, *You Can Quote Me on That* (Dulles, Virginia: Potomac Books, 2005), p. 46.

88 "When do you stop pouring resources into things": Peter Drucker interview with Rich Karlgaard, "Peter Drucker on Leadership," *Forbes.com*, November 19, 2004.

88 "The most dangerous traps for a leader": Ibid.

88 The discussion of Debra Dunn as a young general manager in Hewlett-Packard's test and measurement business was excerpted from Noel Tichy's *The Leadership Engine* (New York: HarperCollins, 1997), pp. 162–63.

89 "I had been involved in building the business": Ibid.

89 "It was very difficult, but it's what I had to do.": Ibid.

89 "If you just envision continuing in the path that you're on": Ibid.

Chapter 8: Working on Your Backhand

92 A good part of the research of this chapter owes its provenance to Jack Zenger and Joseph Folkman's *The Extraordinary Leader* (New York: McGraw-Hill, 2002), including the "halo effect," the key strengths to focus on (e.g., competencies), managerial rankings, and the discussion of "fatal flaws" in managers.

92 "Winning breeds winning": Pete Sampras, *The Tennis Lovers Book of Wisdom (Nashville: Walnut Grove Press, 1997).*

92 "Skill and confidence are not the only determining factors": Paul Fein, *You Can Quote Me on That* (Dulles, Virginia: Potomac Books, 2005), p. 29.

93 Focusing on strengths does not mean making believe that your weaknesses do not exist, "but managing around them": Marcus Buckingham and Donald O. Clifton, *Now Discover Your Strengths* (New York: Simon & Schuster, 2001), p. 148.

94 "Waste as little effort as possible on improving areas of low competence": Peter Drucker, *The Essential Drucker* (New York: Collins Business, 2008), pp. 218–20.

94 "It takes far more energy and far more work to improve from incompetence to low mediocrity": Ibid.

94 They [Buckingham and Clifton] define strength as a "near-perfect performance in an activity": *Now Discover Your Strengths*, pp. 25–26.

94 "Cole Porter's ability to carve the perfect lyric": Ibid.

96 "Be good at 3 or 4 things, not 34 things": Zenger and Folkman, *The Extraordinary Leader,* p. 145.

98   The section on "fatal flaws": Ibid.

101   "The company has a responsibility to 'provide developmental experiences that will provide a positive path to remedy dysfunctional behavior'": Zenger and Folkman, *The Extraordinary Leader*, p. 169.

Chapter 9: Not Getting Enough from Your Coaches

103   "Champions are not born. They are made": Bill Tilden, quoted in Paul Fein, *You Can Quote Me on That* (Dulles, Virginia: Potomac Books, 2005), p. 25.

103   The entire story of Steffi Graf and her father, which included the following quote: "She did not hit the ball and then look around at other things. She was always watching the ball until it was not in play anymore," is excerpted from Martin Schwabacher, *Superstars of Women's Tennis* (Philadelphia: Chelsea House Publishers, 1997), pp. 42–44.

104   "Only those companies that strive to become learning organizations will be prepared to cope": Peter M. Senge, Director, Center for Organizational Learning, Massachusetts Institute of Technology.

105   Roger Enrico's interview granted to author Jeffrey Garten and the quotes that include "There are two things I try to get across," can be found in Jeffrey Garten, *The Mind of the CEO* (New York: Basic Books, 2001), p.149.

106   "Asking a lot of questions opens new doors to new ideas": Michael Dell, *Direct from Dell* (New York: Collins, 1999), p. 123.

108   "Information in its raw form doesn't present itself in neat and tidy packages": Ibid, p. 133.

108 "Random bits of information . . . won't always lead you to the answer": Ibid, pp. 133–34.

110 "everyone teaches, everyone learns": Noel Tichy, *The Cycle of Leadership* (New York: Collins, p. 2002), p.2.

110 having a "teachable point of view" is one of Noel Tichy's seminal concepts. It is described in several of his books, including *The Cycle of Leadership*, p. 11.

110 "leaders must draw appropriate lessons from their experience": Ibid.

Chapter 10: Not Practicing Enough

114 "I have to give Lendl credit. Nobody in the sport as ever worked as hard": John McEnroe, *You Cannot Be Serious* (New York: Putnam, 2002), p. 155.

114 "Through some difficult times, Lendl turned himself into an incredibly tough player": Ibid., p. 156.

115 "the direct result of Lendl's example": Ibid., p. 213.

115 "You know what the name Lendl means": Pete Sampras, quoted in Paul Fein, *You Can Quote Me on That* (Dulles, Virginia: Potomac Books, 2005), p. 85.

118 The discussion of "leading with your out-box" appeared in my previous book, *The Rumsfeld Way* (New York: McGraw-Hill, 2002), p. 58. The concept of "leading with your out-box" is Donald Rumsfeld's brainchild.

Chapter 11: Not Improving Your Game

123 "Progress and improvement do not come in big bunches": Arthur
     Ashe, quoted in Dennis Swanberg, *Man Does Not Live by Sports
     Alone* (New York: Howard Books, 2006), p. 141.

123 "Perfect strokes are already in us, waiting to be discovered":
     W. Timoth, Gallwey, quoted in Criswell Freeman, *The Tennis Lover's
     Book of Wisdom* (Walnut Grove Press, 1997), p. 47.

127 The story of Grove and Moore and viewing their company as outsiders:
     "If we got kicked out and the board brought in a new CEO, what do
     you think he would do?": Ibid., p. 79.

127 "With all the rhetoric about how management is about change": Andy
     Grove, *Only the Paranoid Survive* (New York: Doubleday, 1996),
     p. 123.

128 "Resolution of strategic dissonance does not come in the form of a
     figurative light bulb": Ibid., p. 130.

128 "the level of control that your organization normally is accustomed
     to": Ibid., p. 130.

128 "Let people try different techniques, review different products, exploit
     different sales channels and go after different customers. . . . old ruts
     will bring new insights": Ibid., p. 130.

128 "The dilemma is that you can't suddenly start experimenting when
     you realize you're in trouble": Ibid., p. 130.

129 "The real engine of Google's success is its innovation. Consequently,
     we look to our managers": Steve Tappin and Andrew Cave, *The Secrets
     of CEOs* (London: Nicholas Brealey Publishing, 2008), p. 218.

129 The story of Google's VP Jonathan Rosenberg citing Peter Drucker and looking for "non-traditional savants" is excerpted from the official Google Web site.

130 "Non-routine problems call for non-routine solutions": Ibid.

130 "Don't ditch projects—morph them": Marissa Mayer, Ibid.

Chapter 12: Not Watching the Whole Court

132 "However good your shots": Ken Rosewall, quoted in his book, *Play Tennis with Rosewall: The Little Master and His Method* (Wilshire Book Company, 1975).

133 "To the successful executive in a competitive organization": Dr. Kathleen Reardon, *The Secret Handshake* (New York: Broadway Business, 2002), p. 2.

Epilogue: Beyond the Unforced Error

144 "It takes five years to make a tennis player": Bill Tilden, quoted in Paul Fein, *You Can Quote Me on That* (Dulles, Virginia: Potomac Books, 2005), p. 184.

144 "I am a great believer in practice": Ibid, p. 181.

146 "Being the best in the world is seriously underrated": Seth Godin, *The Dip* (New York: Portfolio, 2007), p. 10.

146 "Anyone who is going to hire you, buy from you, recommend you": Ibid., p. 11.

147 "people who translate mission into results, people who are the basic
     unit of excellence": Charles Garfield, *Peak Performers* (New York:
     William Morrow, 1986), p. 16.

148 "are always willing to evolve and grow, to learn from the work": Ibid.

148 "commitment to one's work is the key source of peak performance":
     Ibid.

148 The research and discussion of "outliers"—those individuals who
     perform at levels far above almost everyone else—are inspired and in
     small bits excerpted from Malcolm Gladwell's book, *Outliers: The
     Story of Success* (New York: Little Brown & Company, 2008).

149 "excellence at performing a complex task requires a critical minimum
     level of practice": Ibid., pp. 39–40.

149 Gladwell's discussion of the Beatles and how they performed some
     1,200 times before coming to the United States and how a decade had
     elapsed from their founding to their best albums: Ibid., pp. 47–50.

150 "a number of researchers now argue that talent means nothing like
     what we think it means": Geoff Colvin, *Talent Is Overrated* (New
     York: Portfolio, 2008), p. 23.

150 "In studies of accomplished individuals, researchers have found few
     signs of precocious achievement": Ibid., p 23.

150 "Deliberate" or "well-structured practice," according to Ericsson, is
     "focused, programmatic, carried out over extended periods of time":
     John Horn and Hiromi Masunaga, *The Cambridge Handbook* (New
     York: Cambridge University Press, 2006), p. 601.

151 "Specific goals are set at successive stages of expertise development.
     It involves appropriate, immediate feedback": Ibid., p. 601.

151 Geoff Colvin's tri-tiered explanation of "deliberate practice" can be found in his book *Talent Is Overrated,* pp. 18–19, 52–53, 63.

152 Ericsson's research showed that the ten years of deliberate practice could take many forms, including "formal education, private instruction, coaching or mentoring": Horn and Masunaga, *The Cambridge Handbook,* p. 327.

153 researchers also agree that "the specific nature of the instruction depends greatly on the type of expertise being acquired": Ibid., p. 327.

153 "For example, outstanding leaders require different educational experiences than do exceptional creators": Ibid.

153 "In field after field, when it came to centrally important skills": Colvin, *Talent Is Overrated,* p. 3.

INDEX